GULF WAR II

OPERATION IRAQI FREEDOM: THE AIR WAR

Jamie Hunter

with Tony Holmes

Published in the UK by TomCat Publishing Ltd
Printed in the UK by Ian Allan Printing Ltd, Hersham, Surrey

ISBN 0-9542191-1-2

2

Front and back cover: **Coalition air power. Front cover photo credits:**
US Navy/USAF/No 617 Squadron/Richard Cooper/
via No 1(F) Squadron/No 617 Squadron/Jamie Hunter
Back cover photo credits: *US Navy/USAF*

Title page: **The Boeing F-15E Strike Eagle formed part of the
awesome array of firepower ready to strike at the Iraqi regime. This
example from the 4th Fighter Wing at Seymour Johnson AFB, SC,
carries an extensive load of GBU-12 Laser Guided Bombs and AIM-9
Sidewinder missiles.** *Lou Drummond*

Contents: **The Coalition – a unique formation of aircraft that operated
from Al Udeid, Qatar, during Operation 'Iraqi Freedom'.** *USAF*

TomCat Publishing
83 The Street, Tongham, Farnham, Surrey,
GU10 1DD, England
www.tomcatpublishing.co.uk

Lead Photography:	Jamie Hunter
Graphic Design:	Philip Hempell
Publisher (UK and worldwide):	TomCat Publishing Ltd
Text:	Jamie Hunter and Tony Holmes Special thanks to Sqn Ldr Gale, RAF, and Flt Lt Turk, RAF
Concept, Editing, Production & Co-ordination:	Richard Cooper
Reproduction:	Ian Allan Printing Ltd
Printing:	Ian Allan Printing Ltd
Edition:	July 2004

Contents

4

AUTHORS' NOTES

The compilation of this book has really underlined the dedication, professionalism and bravery of the men and women of the Coalition armed forces – the people who can be called upon to protect our countries at a moment's notice and put their lives on the line.

Operation 'Iraqi Freedom', Operation 'Telic' and Operation 'Falconer' saw the unprecedented use of precision weaponry to minimise collateral damage and inflict swift blows where it counted most. The opportunity to see these men and women in action and to share some of their experiences and thoughts has been a genuinely humbling experience.

I would personally like to thank Richard Cooper, Peter J. Cooper, Mike Draper and Tony Holmes; Dale Donovan RAF CCO; Brig Gen Hunt 49th FW; Wg Cdr Mark Roberts, Sqn Ldr D'L, Sqn Ldr David Rowe, Sqn Ldr 'Windy' Gale, Sqn Ldr Simon Tickle, Sqn Ldr James, Sqn Ldr Richie Matthews, Flt Lt Andy Turk DFC, Flt Lt Dave Bolsover, Flt Lt Paul Francis RAF; Lt Col Dave Wooden, Lt Col Vraa, Maj John Bryan, Lt Nora Eyle 49th FW; Maj Morgan, Lt Gonzalez 52nd FW PA; Capt Darren Gray 52nd FW; US Navy Sixth Fleet PA; Cdr Wade 'Torch' Knudson, Cdr Tom Bourbeau VX-30; Lt Cdr Hernandez, Lt David Luckett CHINFO; Lt Terry Dudley USNAVEUR; Bob Archer, Greg L. Davis, Lou Drummond, Dylan Eklund, Richard Flagg, Peter R. Foster, Nate Leong and Peter R. March.

Jamie Hunter, Surrey, 2004

I would like to thank Lt Cdr Danny Hernandez and Lt David Luckett of the US Navy's CHINFO News Desk in the Pentagon for granting me access to naval aviators who participated in OIF. COMNAVAIRLANT's Deputy Public Affairs Officer Mike Maus and NAS Lemoore's Public Affairs Officer Dennis McGrath also worked tirelessly on my behalf 'in the field'. Finally, thanks to the pilots and WSOs from the following units, whose OIF experiences and/or photographs are featured in this volume; CVW-8 CAG Capt David Newland, Lt Cdr Mark Weisgerber and Lt Josh Appezzato VFA-41, Lt Cdr Zeno Rausa CVW-2, Lt John Turner VFA-115, Cdr Sean Clark VFA-201, Cdr Doug Denneny VF-2, Cdr Marcus Hitchcock and Lt Dave Dequeljoe VF-32. Lt Col Lee Schram, AV-8B Harrier Co-ordinator Marine Corps HQ. Maj David Rude, Battalion Executive Officer 1st Battalion (Attack), 3rd Aviation Regiment, US Army.

Tony Holmes, Kent, 2004

Foreword

On being asked to write a foreword to this book, my immediate problem was that, as a single member of a 42,000 UK deployment, the view from my cockpit was focussed on a tiny part of the entire air war. The Tornado GR4 force I deployed with was just a small part of a 100-plus fixed-wing and 30 rotary-wing RAF component. Combined with the Royal Navy, Royal Marines and Army Air Corps helicopters, the UK military assets were a fraction of the overall force when compared to the USAF and USN strengths. However, UK air assets were able to cover approximately 10% of the overall tasking. This is partly due to the phenomenal support our ground staff gave us and I wish to take this opportunity to thank them on behalf of all the aircrews for their 'can do' attitude throughout.

As the 'kick-off' approached, the plan (or 'Air Tasking Order') for Day One had been finalised. The complexity of the plan was highlighted by the many hours it took for us to just print out our copy. Many months of contingency planning in the Allied Command Centres produced a timeline of events that was historic in its proportions. Each unit tasked was aware of how it fitted into the 'Commander's Aims' and also, how each of our missions would interact. The 'Shock and Awe' of 21 March was not only limited to those to which it was intended. The view through my Night Vision Goggles of Baghdad below, will remain forever etched on my mind.

The RAF utilised many new technologies and techniques, such as ALARM II, Storm Shadow, as well as the versatile dual role (GPS/Laser Guided) Enhanced Paveway II and III weapons. Close Air Support took up the vast majority of our tasking. Prior to many of these sorties, we were only given an idea of which area we may be subsequently tasked to operate in. The Air Tasking Order would often involve us working closely alongside USAF and RAAF aircraft within the target areas as well as any ground units requiring our support.

The air campaign achieved its aim of supporting the land forces all the way to their objectives. As is the nature of war, all aircrews were subject to significant pressure and danger throughout. Under such intense conditions, mistakes are inevitable and unfortunately the consequences are often tragic. On a personal note, I would like to pass on my sincerest sympathies to the families and friends of Flight Lieutenants Kev Main and Dave Williams.

I hope that the reader takes away an insight into the complexities of the modern air war. No doubt the lessons identified from this conflict will fuel the thesis of many a defence student.

Andy Turk
Flight Lieutenant, DFC RAF

Operation 'Iraqi Freedom'

As a pair of Lockheed Martin F-117A Nighthawks of the USAF's 49th FW slipped into the warm Persian night on 17 March, few people knew that the opening shots of the second Gulf War against Iraq were about to be fired.

Since the end of Operation 'Desert Storm' in 1991, Iraq has been a thorn in the side of the international community. Coalition Forces of the United States and the United Kingdom had been forced to maintain a constant presence in the region to 'keep Saddam Hussein in his cage'. Iraq had constantly dragged its heels over its post-1991 commitment to rid itself of Weapons of Mass Destruction (WMD), with United Nations

Top left: **Five US Navy carrier battle groups headed for the Gulf region, poised for action.** *US Navy*

Centre left: **United States President George W. Bush was ready to deal with Saddam's evil regime. He took a very tough stance from the beginning and set about amassing a formidable military machine to challenge Iraqi defiance.** *US DoD*

Left: **By late February 2003, the Coalition had assembled a huge military presence in the Gulf region ready to tackle Saddam Hussein's regime. Like all Coalition assets, the United States Air Force (USAF) B-1B Lancer is able to strike with pinpoint accuracy.** *USAF*

Bottom left: **Saddam's illicit missile programmes included the development of new al-Samoud II missiles capable of operational ranges exceeding the 94 mile (150km) limit imposed by the UN following the first Gulf War.** *US Navy*

Below: **The 8th Fighter Squadron 'Black Sheep' from Holloman AFB, NM, deployed 12 of its potent F-117A Nighthawks to the Persian Gulf in February 2003.** *Jamie Hunter/aviacom*

(UN) weapons inspectors eventually being thrown out of Iraq in 1998 as the disarmament process ground to a halt.

However, the US 'war on terror' sparked renewed impetus to implement the UN Resolution stating that Iraq had to destroy its WMD. A new Resolution (1441) was agreed in late 2002 stating that time was running out for Saddam and that a new team of UN inspectors should enter Iraq and would require unconditional proof that the country had indeed fulfilled its obligations, or face the consequences.

From an early stage it was clear that the situation inside Iraq was confused. Co-operation with the inspectors was lacking, and the US and UK alliance was losing patience.

As Chief Weapons inspector Dr Hans Blix returned regular reports to the UN throughout early 2003, it was clear that some progress was being made, but not enough in the eyes of US President George W. Bush and the British Prime Minister Tony Blair.

As the two powers made bold moves towards a second Gulf War, China, Germany, and most notably France and Russia, voiced strong objections and made it clear that they would not support military action, making UN backing for war increasingly uncertain. As Iraq continued to cleverly 'drip-feed' co-operation, Saddam Hussein had succeeded in splitting the UN Security Council members.

As of mid-March 2003 the Coalition had amassed a huge military presence in the Gulf region, ready to deliver a lethal strike at an ill-equipped, yet unpredictable Iraqi military regime. This strike was to be swift and powerful to remove Saddam Hussein from power and rid Iraq of its alleged chemical and biological weapons once and for all. The countdown to war was on.

The move to war

The start of 2003 saw the United States and United Kingdom remain insistent that Saddam Hussein and his evil regime harboured Weapons of Mass Destruction (WMD) and even links to the Al Qaeda terror network, rendering him an intolerable threat. Evidence was produced to suggest that Iraq was concealing chemical weapons, with the Coalition only being satisfied if Saddam complied with UN resolutions to the letter.

Around that time President Bush commented; 'Evidence from intelligence sources, secret communications, and statements by people now in custody, reveal that Saddam

Left: **The USS *Abraham Lincoln* (CVN-72) and its Carrier Air Wing Fourteen (CVW-14) was on its way back home when it was recalled to the Gulf in preparation for possible military action.** *US Navy*

Inset: **President George W. Bush and Defense Secretary Donald Rumsfeld piled the pressure on Iraqi leader Saddam Hussein to come clean on all his illegal weapons programmes. As the Iraqi leader stalled, the Coalition prepared for military action.** *US DoD*

Below left: **During early 2003, USAF assets deployed to the region were kept busy flying Operation 'Northern Watch' and 'Southern Watch' missions over Iraq, with regular hostile ground fire. These F-16s are seen returning to Prince Sultan AB in Saudi Arabia.** *USAF*

Below: **The huge military build-up included a large deployment from the Royal Air Force (RAF). This included VC10 C1K tankers and Tornado GR4s as seen here en-route to forward operating bases.** *No 12(B) Squadron*

Sequence: **The first Tornados from No IX(B) Squadron left RAF Marham on 10 February for 'Telic' duties.** *Richard Cooper*

Hussein aids and protects terrorists, including members of Al Qaeda'. US Secretary of State, Colin Powell, told the United Nations Security Council it 'should not be scared into impotence when it came to dealing with Iraq'.

However, the case for war remained far from sold to all UN delegates. UN chief weapons inspector Dr Hans Blix reported on 27 January that, in the first two months of inspections in Iraq, the regime had complied reluctantly and that Saddam may still possess biological weapons and rockets. Blix was sharply critical of the Iraqi regime stating that it might still have stocks of anthrax, and that Saddam had failed to account for up to 300 rocket engines. However, the head of the International Atomic Energy Agency, Mohamed El Baradei, said his inspectors had found no evidence that Iraq had resumed its nuclear programme it discontinued in the early 1990s.

Meanwhile, NATO quarrelled over the desire to reinforce Turkey's air defence network, with concerns raised over deep divisions within the alliance. With a deal struck, however, the Supreme Allied Commander Europe, Gen James L. Jones, acted quickly and ordered NATO E-3 AWACS to deploy to Konya AB in Turkey as a matter of urgency to aid the defensive measures to assist the country.

Despite the NATO agreement on improved defences, Turkish-US relations failed to pave the way for US troops to deploy to the country for a potential invasion of Iraq from the north. The US Army's 3rd Infantry Division and the US Marine Corps' 1st Marine Division were poised to move in from Kuwait in the south, with the US wanting to deploy the Army's 4th

COMMAND AND CONTROL

Headquartered at MacDill AFB, FL, United States Central Command (USCENTCOM) is one of nine Unified Combatant Commands that control US combat forces, and was the command set to oversee the action in the Persian Gulf. CENTCOM is composed of six Component Commands: USARCENT (Army), USCENTAF (Air Force), USMARCENT (Marines), USNAVCENT (Navy), SOCCENT (Special Ops) and NORTHCOM (Homeland Defense). Commanding CENTCOM was General Tommy R. Franks, reporting directly to the US Defense Secretary Donald Rumsfeld, who in turn reports to President George W. Bush.

CENTCOM's Area of Responsibility (AOR) stretches from 'The Horn of Africa' to Central Asia. It functions as a headquarters for US forces but has no frontline units permanently assigned. Instead, the armed services provide CENTCOM with 'component commands' that make up its primary combat capability. With General Franks at the helm, CENTCOM prepared to run the show.

Inset: **General Tommy R. Franks, the Commander of Operation 'Iraqi Freedom'.** *CENTCOM*

Below: **The heart of the operation, the Combined Air Operations Centre (CAOC) remained in Saudi Arabia, with CENTCOM headquarters at Camp Doha, Qatar.** *CENTCOM*

Heavy transport aircraft, such as RAF and USAF Boeing C-17s, worked around the clock to haul supplies and equipment out to the operational theatre. By mid-February, the USAF had deployed 250,000 additional troops to within striking distance of Iraq. *Crown Copyright/USAF*

Infantry Division in Turkey, but this never happened and Turkey stood firm against the plan for war.

Weapons inspectors Hans Blix and Muhammad El Baredi reported back to the UN security council on 14 February and, despite outlining several key issues that still contravened UN Resolution 1441, said that Iraq was co-operating more and that real progress was being made. Dr Blix opened with a summary of weapons inspections (400 inspection missions in 11 weeks), and he noted Iraqi co-operation in the process of these inspections. Crucially though, he added that many weapons and items were still not accounted for. He later stated that while serious questions did still remain, notably the disappearance of large quantities of chemical and biological material – definite progress had been made with inspections, fuelling the case for more time to be given to inspectors.

Dr Blix presented information on two variants of the controversial al-Samoud missile, with the al-Samoud II being capable of operational ranges exceeding the 94 mile (150km) limit imposed by the UN following the Gulf War in 1991. Iraq was instructed to cease this programme and destroy the missiles, which it belatedly set about doing so.

It was still not enough. On 22 February, US Defense Secretary Donald Rumsfeld warned Saddam that all military assets were in place and that the United States was ready for war.

Iraq responded to the threat on 9 March by declaring that it was free of Weapons of Mass Destruction at its weekly press conference in Baghdad. The announcement was quickly dismissed by America and Britain. Saddam hurriedly put Iraq on a war footing, ordering the country to be split into four military zones. Defences around the major cities were reportedly boosted and then, on 17 March, President Bush issued a stark warning to Saddam Hussein that gave him 48hrs to leave Iraq or face military action.

War Diary

(see page 25)

PREPARING FOR WAR

The Coalition military build-up was huge, with US, British and Australian forces ready for action from bases around Iraq. The US military had bolstered its already impressive might in the region, while the British Forces also committed massive resources and around 42,000 personnel as the Coalition moved onto a war footing. Waves of USAF C-5 Galaxys, C-17 Globemasters, C-130 Hercules and C-141 Starlifters hauled personnel and equipment to the region as the build-up reached its peak in late February 2003.

The USAF's Expeditionary Air and Space Force (EAF) came into its own, with EAF7 and EAF8 having deployed in November 2002 with upwards of 1,000 USAF combat aircraft in theatre poised to strike. The US Civil Reserve Air Fleet (CRAF) had also been activated on 8 February to mobilise 47 long-haul airliners from 11 carriers to facilitate the movement of 150,000 American troops to the Gulf. The US Navy had five carrier battle groups, the US Marine Corps had at least four assault carriers and the Royal Navy had carrier HMS *Ark Royal* on station. The US Marines had moved the entire 1st and 2nd Marine Expeditionary Forces (MEF) from bases in California and North Carolina aboard one of the largest amphibious forces assembled since WW2. Meanwhile, helicopters from the US Army and US Marine Corps and the British Army, Royal Marines and Australian Army moved alongside the ground forces and set up forward area refuelling and re-arming points (FARPs) actually inside the Iraqi borders.

On station and ready for action. A US Navy F-14D Tomcat of VF-213 'Black Lions', part of CVW-8 embarked on the USS Theodore Roosevelt (CVN-71) in the Mediterranean in mid-March. *Jamie Hunter/aviacom*

Sky News was the first to report the dramatic developments. At 05.34hrs local time on 20 March 2003, aircraft and cruise missiles attacked targets in and around Baghdad – Operation 'Iraqi Freedom' had begun. The name (which was commonly abbreviated to OIF) was adopted by the US Department of Defense, with Operations 'Telic' (derived from the Greek word for 'purposeful') and 'Falconer' used by the UK and Australian Ministries of Defence respectively.

The conflict's opening shots were aimed directly at Saddam Hussein during a 'target of opportunity' attack that was designed as a decapitation strike at the heart of the Iraqi leadership (see page 25). A response came in the form of two 'Scud-type' missiles and two 'anti-shipping' missiles being fired at targets in Kuwait. One missile was headed for the Kuwaiti capital but was intercepted by a US Patriot missile, with at least two other missiles landing in the desert, reportedly near a US Marine Corps land base. This prompted a succession of chemical and biological weapon alerts for the coalition forces stationed in the northern Kuwaiti desert as fears of Saddam's unpredictable warfare capabilities were played out.

Coalition forces began the 'main offensive' on the evening of 20 March by launching an artillery barrage that was followed by air strikes in southern Iraq and Baghdad. The Baghdad attacks saw Coalition aircraft employing precision-guided weapons to smash Iraqi command and communications positions with pinpoint accuracy, causing minimal collateral damage.

As the conflict got into full pace on 21 March, more than 1,000 sorties were flown against several hundred targets throughout Iraq while US and British warships and submarines fired over 400 Tomahawk cruise missiles against fixed targets – this was the start of what was famously labelled the 'Shock and Awe' attacks. Some 100 conventional air-launched cruise missiles (CALCM) were also launched and coalition aircraft delivered around 700 precision-guided munitions. While air support missions were flown from about 30 bases throughout the Persian Gulf region (as well as the five US Navy aircraft carriers), the majority of the USAF heavy bomber force began operations from forward-deployed locations. Indeed, B-52H Stratofortresses flew from bases as far away as RAF Fairford in

Gloucestershire, UK, while B-2A Spirits conducted 34hr round trips from their home base at Whiteman AFB, MO.

Sooner than expected, ground troops began an immediate offensive into Iraq. Upon entering the country, US Marines and British Commandos set about taking the Al Faw peninsula as the US Army 3rd Infantry Division and the 1st Marine Division engaged Iraqi ground forces and spearheaded the push north.

The crucial first week at war

DAY 1 | 20 March

- US Marines, US Navy SEALs and British Royal Marines of 3, 40 and 42 Commando worked swiftly from the outset of combat operations to take the crucial Al Faw peninsula with a massive aerial and amphibious assault. The offensive was launched from ships in the Persian Gulf with US Marine Corps CH-46 and CH-53s working alongside British Joint Helicopter Command (JHC) Chinook HC2s and Sea King HC4s. This was followed by an assault on the port town of Umm Qasr, which proved a tough target with sporadic resistance from Iraqi troops.
- USAF, US Navy, US Marine Corps and RAF aircraft supported the advancing ground troops by undertaking Close Air Support (CAS) missions as well as the striking of Iraqi military installations to sever the Iraqi chain of command and communications. RAF Tornado GR4As and Harrier

GR7s flew 'Scud Hunt' missions in the western desert as well as CAS missions armed with AGM-65 Mavericks, RBL-755s and Enhanced Paveway IIs.

- Around 72 cruise missiles were launched at strategic targets from US Navy ships as well as Royal Navy submarines HMS *Turbulent* and HMS *Splendid*.
- US Army AH-64Ds and US Marine Corps AH-1Ws were employed against pockets of Iraqi resistance including Armoured Personnel Carriers (APCs) and tanks as ground forces 'probed forwards'.
- Air attacks were reported on the northern Iraqi city of Mosul. Reports came through of US and UK Special Forces cutting makeshift airstrips in the surrounding area.
- Iraqis torched seven oil wells and 'booby trapped' others as Coalition forces worked to secure Iraq's most valuable asset for its people in the future.
- US Army 3rd Infantry Division and V Corps 'sprinted' north across the Iraqi desert towards An Nassiriya.
- Prime Minister Tony Blair made a statement to say that the mission was 'to remove Saddam Hussein from power and disarm Iraq of its weapons of mass destruction'.

Below: **Waves of strike aircraft departed from the five US Navy aircraft carriers in the Mediterranean and the Persian Gulf headed for Iraq. This VMFA-115 'Silver Eagles' F/A-18C Hornet seen blasting out from the USS** *Harry S. Truman* **(CVN-75).** *US Navy*

DAY 2 21 March

- Eight USAF B-52Hs launched from RAF Fairford in the late morning and headed for Iraq.
- British troops pushed towards the key southern city of Basra. Some US troops already 100 miles into Iraq at this stage.
- Remote western H2 and H3 airfields were captured.
- Massive 'Shock and Awe' air strikes began after dark. Baghdad was rocked by colossal explosions as the air war began in earnest. Action dubbed 'A-Day' by the US administration. Air strikes were carefully planned to avoid infrastructure damage and target the Iraqi leadership regime.
- Big SEAD 'push' around Baghdad. US Navy EA-6Bs, USAF F-16CJs and RAF Tornados tackled Air Defence capabilities around the Iraqi capital. RAF Tornado GR4s also attacked facilities around Kirkuk. Around 1,000 sorties flown by the end of the night, with 80 being by the RAF.

DAY 3 22 March

- Two Royal Navy Sea King ASAC7s of 849NAS collided near HMS *Ark Royal* in the early morning. Six Royal Navy crewmembers and a US observer lost their lives.
- British minesweepers were engaged in clearing the port at Umm Qasr, ready for the humanitarian relief effort.
- Basra Airport taken by British Royal Marines. The city itself was not entered at this stage in an attempt to avoid Fighting In Built Up Area (FIBUA).
- B-52s launched from RAF Fairford at midnight, for daylight raids over Iraq using GBU-31 JDAMs.
- An MQ-1 Predator located a ZSU-23-4 mobile radar-directed anti-aircraft gun utside the southern town of Al Amarah, and destroyed it using a single AGM-114K Hellfire II missile. Significantly, it was the first drone 'kill' of the conflict.

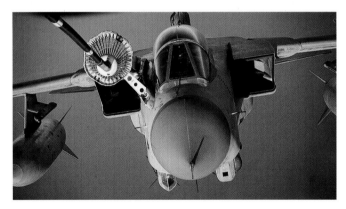

Top: **The menacing Northrop Grumman B-2A Spirit. The USAF deployed four Stealth bombers to Diego Garcia as part of the 40th Air Expeditionary Wing, as well as flying missions direct from home base at Whiteman AFB, MO.** *USAF*

Above: **As the sun sets, an RAF Tornado GR4 plugs in to a USAF KC-10 Extender. The aircraft is part of a late night strike package heading into Iraq.** *Lou Drummond*

DAY 4 23 March

- RAF Tornado GR4 from No IX(B) Squadron shot down in error by a US Patriot missile in a friendly fire incident ('Blue on Blue'). The aircraft was one of a pair returning from a SEAD combat mission over Iraq. Both the pilot and the navigator were killed.
- Fierce fighting continued around Umm Qasr, Najaf and An Nassiriya as US and British ground forces continued to head north. US Marine Corps F/A-18s and RAF Harrier GR7s provided Close Air Support (CAS) around Umm Qasr, the port town that still held 'pockets of resistance'.

DAY 5 24 March

- Fighting continued around Umm Qasr, Najaf and An Nassiriya as Iraqi Republican Guard forces that had been moved into the area proved hard to contain. Iraqis employed guerrilla-style tactics as well as soldiers masquerading as civilians or pretending to surrender before opening fire.
- US Army AH-64D (99-5135) of 1-227 Avn from Fort Hood, TX, was shown on Iraqi TV having force-landed in a field near Najaf. Reports suggest this Apache was one of around 40 examples that attacked Republican Guard positions south of Baghdad. The two US Army aircrew were captured and shown on Iraqi TV. The Apache was later attacked and destroyed by US forces to prevent the Iraqi military from taking the helicopter.
- Some 6,000 US and 1,600 RAF missions were reported as having been flown since combat operations began.
- RAAF F/A-18A Hornets flew attack missions over Iraq. Australian Special Forces also reported to be 'on the ground' in the country.
- Iraqi 'Frog' missiles were fired at Kuwait. Missiles were either destroyed by US Patriots or fell onto open land.

DAY 6 25 March

- The US military reported that Iraq had been using six GPS jamming systems acquired from a 'foreign nation' – probably Russia. These were employed in an attempt to spoof GPS-guided weapons. All six systems were reportedly destroyed by high priority air strikes – the last using a GPS-guided weapon!
- Severe sandstorms swept across the region, but operations continued at an impressive pace.

DAY 7 26 March

- The ground forces pushed further into Iraq at a rapid rate, supported by the huge air armada that was able to operate with total air supremacy.
- Close Air Support (CAS) air strikes on Republican Guard positions south of Baghdad by RAF Harrier GR7s and USAF A-10s and B-52s softened up the Iraqi defences for the land forces to make headway.

The war continues

The dramatic first week of the offensive had seen a crushing push north by Coalition ground forces, supported by overwhelming airpower launched from bases in the region.

Gen Richard Myers, chairman of the Joint Chiefs of Staff warned 'The war effort won't be quick or easy'. President George W. Bush also warned against expectations of an easy victory. During a visit to US Central Command headquarters at MacDill AFB, FL, he pledged: 'This war is far from over. We will stay on the path, mile by mile, all the way to Baghdad and all the way to victory. Day by day, Saddam Hussein is losing his grip on Iraq. Day by day, the Iraqi people are closer to freedom'.

On the frontline, British Royal Marines initially set about securing the port of Umm Qasr to make way for humanitarian supplies for the needy Iraqi population. Other

Above: **Heading into action – an RAF Tornado GR4 clutches a pair of GPS/laser-guided Enhanced Paveway II bombs as it heads north into Iraqi airspace.** *No 617 Squadron*

Below: **The RC-135W 'Rivet Joint' is an intelligence collection specialist, with a total of nine having deployed for Operation 'Iraqi Freedom'.** *Derek Pedley*

Above: **Looking for action, a US Navy F/A-18C refuels from a USAF KC-135E of the 163rd ARW over Northern Iraq. This Hornet carries a typically diverse load of a Joint Direct Attack Munition (JDAM) and a GBU-12 laser-guided bomb.** *US Navy*

elements of the British Army and Royal Marines headed for Iraq's second city – Basra.

Meanwhile, the US 3rd Infantry Division and the 1st Marine Division speared north towards the ultimate challenge of capturing Baghdad from under the noses of the Iraqi regime. Towns and cities such as An Nassiriyah, Najaf and Karbala were daily talking points as US troops met sporadic but sometimes fierce resistance from troops loyal to Saddam, desperate to close the Coalition's route to the capital. But the push northwards was simply overwhelming in pace and power, with the Iraqi Army left in tatters.

To the north of the country, the failure of the Turkish government to allow Coalition forces to operate from bases inside its country caused a revision to plans for opening a second front in Northern Iraq. As a result, an incredible force of 15 USAF Boeing C-17A Globemaster IIIs air-dropped personnel into Kurdish-held territory on 27 March as part of what was dubbed 'the largest airborne assault since D-Day'. This also marked the first-ever C-17 combat insertion of paratroopers, just one of the many aviation 'firsts' of this conflict.

Supplementing the fighting force, more than 1,000 soldiers from the 173rd Airborne Brigade in Italy brought in specialist skills, ranging from intelligence, medical, communications, security and engineers to name a few.

Over the following five days the USAF conducted 62 airlift flights and delivered 2,000 personnel, more than 400 vehicles and 3,000 tons of supplies to captured airfields in northern Iraq to support the push south towards Mosul, Iraq's third city.

Centre left: **Lining up on Runway 11 at RAF Mildenhall ready to head south for the Gulf, this Boeing E-3B was one of 19 Sentry Airborne Warning and Control Systems (AWACS) that were in the thick of the action from 'night one'.** *Jamie Hunter/aviacom*

Left: **A pilot assigned to VFA-113 'Stingers' enters Iraqi airspace in an F/A-18 Hornet during OIF on 28 March. The unit was embarked aboard USS Abraham Lincoln (CVN-72) with CVW-14.** *US Navy*

To the south, the embedded media reported potential complications with the long supply chain that stretched from Kuwait right up to the frontline – rapidly advancing towards Baghdad. On 28 March, the US military announced the deployment of an additional 120,000 troops to join the operation. However, commanders were quick to stress that this had been planned from 'Day One' and was not to be 'read into' as being a sign that the war wasn't going as planned.

The frontline ground troops were sustained not only through ground assets, but also from the use of hastily prepared desert airstrips that were used as forward operating bases for helicopters and C-130 transports. The Hercules also utilised the former Iraqi AF base at Tallil, which was dubbed 'George Bush International', as a major forward hub to supply the frontlines. RAF C-130Js ferried US troops into the base, ready to move up and join the advance. Furthermore, both assault and support helicopters assisted the troops through air cover and re-supply, underlining the huge advantage of total air supremacy enjoyed by the Coalition. It wasn't long before USAF A-10 Thunderbolt IIs moved in to operate from this austere base.

The remarkable progress by ground forces wasn't without its complications however. On 29 March, a suicide bomber attacked a US Vehicle Control Point (VCP) and killed four US soldiers. This underlined just how risky the whole operation was, and was a clear example of how difficult it was for Coalition troops to differentiate between hostile paramilitaries and innocent civilians. Concerns over more attacks like this were well founded, with further incidents following at checkpoints around the country, and at least one further suicide attack at a VCP.

With the main purpose of the war being to rid Iraq of its oppressive regime and its Weapons of Mass Destruction (WMD), huge emphasis was placed on a number of finds around Iraq. Some of these turned out to be over-eager reporting, but a significant number did appear to indicate that the regime had indeed been in collusion with known terrorist groups and may have also concealed WMD. Reports of the discovery of a 'massive' terrorist base on 30 March were followed by news of a possible mobile chemical weapons laboratory, providing some clues that the pre-war claims were well founded.

The push for Baghdad

As news of an 'operational pause' came from journalists on the frontline, it quickly became clear that this only referred to selected units taking well-earned breaks as the Coalition 'shaped the battlespace' in preparation for the assault on the Iraqi capital – Saddam's last stronghold.

On 2 April, the US Army's 3rd Infantry Division swept past Karbala in an 'armoured dash' towards Baghdad. Supported by a large force of AH-64D Apache attack helicopters, the division moved through the 'Karbala Gap' as it engaged the Iraqi Republican Guard's Medina Division for the last time.

Reports concerning the Baghdad Division of the Republican Guard claimed that it had been totally 'destroyed' and rendered ineffective as a result of punishing air strikes from RAF and US aircraft in engagements near Al Kut. The US Marines 1st MEF advanced north towards the Republican Guard's Nebuchadnezzar Division from the southeastern flank, with the divisions being effectively pinned down in dug-in positions and therefore unable to retreat into Baghdad.

Interestingly, the Republican Guard was banned from Baghdad by Saddam Hussein due to his fears over previous 'coup' attempts by its officers. Only the loyal 'Special' Republican Guard was allowed in the Iraqi capital, but, as the assault on Baghdad gathered pace, these forces seemed to have either been destroyed or just 'melted away'.

By 3 April, the US Army 3rd Infantry Division was reported as being just six miles south of Baghdad and closing in on the strategic goal of Saddam International Airport. Elsewhere, Special Forces mounted assaults on key regime targets, including Saddam's Presidential Palaces, as Coalition fighters changed tactics to ensure 24hr coverage right above the city.

The main assault on Baghdad began in earnest on 4 April as the US Army 3rd Infantry Division moved in on the airport and eventually secured most of it. This was quickly set up as a Forward Operating Base (FOB), with supplies and troops flown in within days aboard C-130s and C-17s.

Right: Bombed up. The first stage of the air campaign saw a massive effort from all aspects of the Coalition force. Here USAF armourers load a GBU-31 JDAM onto an F-16. *USAF*

Below: A pair of 77th FS 'Gamblers' F-16CJs prepare to launch, as a pair of RAF Tornado F3s of No 111 Squadron depart in the background. The F-16s carry a typical Suppression of Enemy Air Defence (SEAD) loadout with AGM-88 HARM missiles. *Crown Copyright*

Above: Precision strike – a bomb entry hole at a Presidential Palace illustrates shows just how accurate Coalition strikes were. USAF

Right: Coalition force – escorted by a pair of RAF Tornado F3s, a USAF B-1B Lancer takes-on fuel from a KC-10A as the 'package' heads into Iraq. USAF

Below: An F-117A Nighthawk from the 8th Expeditionary Fighter Squadron returns from a night strike as a trio of F-15E Strike Eagles from the 4th Fighter Wing launch for daylight missions. These assets, along with F-16CJs and other support types formed the impressive 379th Air Expeditionary Wing at Al Udeid, Qatar. Visible in the background are RAAF F/A-18A Hornets and RAF Tornado GR4s, which were also deployed to the base. USAF

The US Marine Corps headed across southern Baghdad and eventually linked up with Army units following a two-pronged 'pincer' movement from the southeast and southwest of the city – heading for the ultimate goal of the centre of the capital.

News of a major incursion into central Baghdad early on 5 April was seen as a test of the city's defences, a reconnaissance mission to see where they could go. The troop 'drives' through Baghdad were monitored in real-time by USAF UAVs on station overhead, allowing commanders to see just how effective the operations were proving to be.

Meanwhile, out in the Persian Gulf, a sixth US Navy carrier battle group joined operations on 7 April when the USS Nimitz (CVN-68) arrived in the Fifth Fleet AOR. This allowed the USS Abraham Lincoln (CVN-72) to head home after its lengthy deployment.

Securing the country

After playing a probing and waiting game around Iraq's second city of Basra, three formations of British ground forces pushed for the centre of the city as US troops took Baghdad to the north. The UK's Scots Dragoon Guards, Royal Fusiliers and Black Watch soldiers moved quickly, partly spurred on by reports that the military commander for the area (known as 'Chemical Ali' for his warfare track record) had been killed in an air strike.

US Forces spearheaded more incursions into Baghdad centre and faced some stiff resistance, but nothing like as severe as had been expected. A bold move to take control of a Presidential Palace on the banks of the Tigris River enabled US troops to take up residence right in the heart of the capital – the regime had fled.

Left: Returning to its forward operating base at RAF Akrotiri, a 100th ARW KC-135R returns from an Operation 'Iraqi Freedom' mission having provided precious fuel to a US Navy strike package. *USAF*

Astonishing scenes followed on 9 April, as the city erupted into hysteria and Iraqi civilians filled the streets to tear down statues of Saddam. By now the final pockets of Iraqi resistance were pushed back to the eastern part of the city. The battle for Baghdad had been predicted by some as being a potentially difficult and a devastating last stand for Saddam and his henchmen. However in reality it resulted in some 'sporadic' resistance from pockets of loyal Republican Guard, Ba'ath Party and Fedayeen fighters, but with a lack of control this was quickly overcome. Baghdad had fallen.

On 10 April, the northern Iraqi town of Kirkuk fell to Kurdish fighters, sparking concern from Turkey over ties with the city. However, Turkey was sternly told it could only have expected this as it failed to allow US troops in the region.

In Basra, people filled the streets. The overwhelming theme was 'Saddam has gone – now we can live again'. This joy was somewhat short-lived though, with attention quickly turning to the needs of the nation and also how to tackle the mass looting that had rapidly blighted the country's 'liberation'. It became increasingly clear that international assistance was needed fast to help get Iraq back on its feet. Electricity and water supplies had all suffered from the conflict, and law and order needed to be re-established as troops struggled to deal with civilian as well as military issues. The Iraqi police force was encouraged to get back to work and restore order amid increasing unrest due to lack of provisions and the extreme levels of continued looting of buildings, from government establishments to hospitals.

Like a house of cards, after Baghdad 'fell' to US Forces, the remaining key cities to the north offered little resistance. Mosul was declared as being in Coalition hands on 11 April and, by 14 April, US troops had moved into what was thought to be the regime's final stand at Tikrit. This was described by US Central Command (CENTCOM) as the last area of warfighting in Iraq, with operations moving away from combat and edging towards getting Iraq back on its feet.

Gen Richard Myers, chairman of the USAF Joint Chiefs of Staff, pointed out on 15 April that while major combat operations were finished in Iraq, US and coalition forces continued to run into pockets of regime diehards – the battle was over, but the war was still to be won.

As Coalition forces fanned out across Iraq, new reports of regime discoveries emerged. Special Forces reportedly came across a handful of 'small aircraft covered with camouflage' on Highway 1 between Tikrit and Mosul. CENTCOM commented that these could have been used by regime leaders to try to escape, or for the delivery of WMD.

Above: US Army paratroopers and USAF tactical air controllers from the 173rd Airborne Brigade prepare to board USAF C-17A Globemaster IIIs ready for the massive combat insertion into a Kurdish-controlled base. This paved the way to open a spearhead south towards Mosul. *USAF*

Left: A British Army 1st Battalion, Royal Fusiliers soldier keeps guard as a Queen's Royal Lancers Challenger 2 tank advances into southern Iraq. *Crown Copyright*

Below left: The severe sandstorms that hit the region on 25 March did hamper air operations but many continued, most notably USAF E-8 J-STARS missions providing vital information on Iraqi troop movements to ground units. This F-15C Eagle is seen undergoing an engine ground run in the thick sand at Prince Sultan AB. Despite the inclement weather, around 1,500 sorties were flown on 26 March. *USAF*

Below: British and US troops pushed north into Iraq at an impressive rate. These troops are from the 1st Battalion, the Royal Irish Regiment, and are seen patrolling an area near a burning Iraqi oil well. *Crown Copyright*

CENTCOM's Maj Gen Brooks said that US forces had also secured 12 Surface to Air Missiles and six VIP helicopters found near a Ba'ath Party HQ building. CNN showed pictures of a military 'Huey' (understood to be an AB212) under camouflage netting alongside a number of luxury vehicles, including several Rolls-Royce cars. Brooks also said that the Coalition had 'found buried airplanes – MiG fighters'. These turned out to be a ragged collection of MiG-25 'Foxbats' recce/interceptors and Su-25 'Frogfoot' fighter-bombers found by Australian Special Forces and US troops (see later chapter). This information, according to Maj Gen Brooks, supports claims made to international media that the 'Iraqi regime was practiced in deception and denial operations'. He said; 'If the Iraqis were motivated to bury aircraft, they could easily do likewise with WMD'.

But what of Saddam? Many had predicted that he would make that one final stand in his hometown of Tikrit, but he had fled.

Top: **Bashur airfield in northern Iraq was quickly reinforced with equipment and supplies for the push south towards Baghdad. Here US Marine Corps CH-46E Sea Knights and CH-53E Sea Stallions are seen ferrying in Marines from the 26th Marine Expeditionary Unit (MEU).** *USAF*

Inset: **The USAF C-17 fleet was kept busy re-supplying the most austere newly captured bases, including this base in northern Iraq. Note the USAF Special Operations MH-53M Pave Low IVs in the background.** *USAF*

Top right: **As troops pushed north, cities had to be entered and secured. By 5 April, US forces started ground incursions into Baghdad, with the capital falling shortly afterwards.** *US Navy*

Right: **Supporting the push north towards Baghdad, this Fairchild A-10A Thunderbolt II is seen arriving at the captured Iraqi airfield at Tallil on 3 April to join the 392nd Air Expeditionary Wing.** *USAF*

Above: An impressive line-up of USAF C-130 Hercules on the 485th AEW ramp at a forward operating base. This line up was comprised of seven units and represented the largest ever collection of 'Herks' according to USAF officials. *USAF*

Inset: The US Army AH-64 Apache force flew missions around the clock in support of the US Army push north into central Iraq. The dusty conditions provided huge challenges for Army aviators, making all mission phases tricky. *Richard Cooper*

Right: A USAF F-16CJ pilot moves in to refuel from a USAF KC-135R. Note that the pilot wears a combat vest packed with survival equipment should an emergency arise over enemy territory.
Jamie Hunter/aviacom

United States Air Force

FIRST STRIKE: F-117 Nighthawk

As with 'Desert Storm' in 1991 it fell to the Lockheed Martin F-117A Nighthawk to deliver the opening shots of the campaign against the Iraqi regime under Operation 'Iraqi Freedom' (OIF).

Lt Col David Toomey and Maj Mark Hoehn of the 8th FS 'Black Sheep' from the 49th FW at Holloman AFB, NM, were tasked with the critical first mission at very short notice. On 19 March, even before the air campaign had started, the two pilots received details of an ultra secret and time-sensitive mission to be flown against the senior Iraqi leadership, which Intelligence had discovered were occupying a compound in the Dora Farms complex near Baghdad. The pilots, who were assigned to the 379th Air Expeditionary Wing at Al Udeid AB, Qatar, were tasked with launching the 'decapitation' strike less than two hours after being notified, with minimal planning material available.

Maj Clint Hinote, a Nighthawk pilot deployed as a mission planner on Lt Gen Michael Moseley's Combined Air Forces Component staff, sat in the dining facility chatting with friends and fellow pilots. A few minutes before, he had briefed Moseley on plans for the first few days of the pending air war. 'I was pretty tired and taking a break when one of the guys from the Time Sensitive Targeting (TST) cell came in and told me I was needed back on the planning floor', Hinote recalled. 'When I got there, I was told we needed to get two jets ready for a strike on a leadership position. The word had come directly from the Pentagon'.

Above: **When commanders needed to mount a vital 'decapitation' strike on 19 March 2003, they turned to the F-117A detachment from the 8th Expeditionary Fighter Squadron. As dawn broke, a pair of Nighthawks piloted by Lt Col David Toomey and Maj Mark Hoehn slipped into Iraqi airspace ready to deliver the first precision strikes of Operation 'Iraqi Freedom'.** *Jamie Hunter/aviacom*

Below: **An F-117A Nighthawk of the 8th EFS seen over the Persian Gulf on 14 April, shortly before returning to its home base at Holloman AFB, NM. Note the mission marks below the cockpit.** *USAF*

Above: **With brake chute billowing, an 8th EFS F-117A taxies back to its shelter at Al Udeid where the Nighthawks operated as part of the 379th Air Expeditionary Wing.** *USAF*

Above right: **Maj Mark Hoehn returned to Holloman AFB, NM, in April following his significant contribution to OIF. He was later awarded the Distinguished Flying Cross (DFC).** *USAF*

The intelligence had indicated that Saddam Hussein and his two sons Uday and Qusai were in the bunker at the rarely-used palace complex in Dora Farms, in suburban Baghdad. A successful strike could decapitate the Iraqi military leadership and dramatically shorten the campaign.

Short-notice strikes are not usual practice for the F-117 community, with the Nighthawk being optimised for special missions, requiring comprehensive lead-in planning. A normal F-117 mission planning cycle can start anything up to 20 hours prior to the final attack – so the clock was well and truly ticking as, this time, the pilots had just four hours. These short-notice orders became known as 'Silver Bullet' missions, for which the F-117 had become the planner's number one choice.

On top of the time schedule, the urgency meant that the F-117s would be over target just after 05.00hrs – the rising sun over Baghdad would uncloak these masters of the night and expose them to anti-aircraft fire. The F-117 can hide from Surface-to-Air Missiles (SAMs) but not from visually aimed triple-A (Anti-Aircraft Artillery, or AAA).

Hoehn and Toomey were swift into action, not only would they be the first into enemy airspace, but they would also be using a new weapon – the GPS-guided EGBU-27 Enhanced Paveway III bunker-buster. 'The maintenance area was a swarm of activity', Hoehn recalled. 'They wanted to pull it off as much as we did. Those guys, maintenance, munitions, support, just teamed up and made miracles happen'.

'The munitions had to be dropped two at a time', Hoehn continued. 'We didn't know if that would work. They could collide with each other or tumble off course. We simply didn't know what this munition did. It was a little nerve-wracking'.

With their Nighthawks ready, the pilots headed out into the dark Persian night using the callsigns 'Ram 01/02'. The escorts were also getting airborne in the shape of two US Navy EA-6B Prowlers and a pair of USAF F-16CJs as well as the all-important tankers. A further Prowler from the USS *Constellation* (CV-64) in the Persian Gulf joined the package as the seven aircraft met up at the KC-135s. As they neared the Iraqi border, the tanker turned back, with the Prowlers and F-16s staying with the F-117s for a while longer before allowing the two Stealths to slip into Baghdad airspace alone.

As 'Ram 01' and 'Ram 02' headed for Baghdad, the morning sun was rising – not a good time for a Nighthawk to be waging war. 'At altitude, it gets very bright', Hoehn said. 'We needed to get to the target quickly'.

The pair ducked under a wave of broken clouds over the target and opened the bomb bay doors at the last possible moment, making the Nighthawk visible to radar over an area that had over 50 SAM systems and more than 200 triple-A sites defending it.

As the pilots released their weapons a rain of Tomahawk cruise missiles also hit home around the city in a well-timed and heavy-hitting attack.

Soon after the Nighthawks had peeled away from the target the first of a series of explosions tore the compound apart and the triple-A batteries started their retaliation.

The Stealth pilots received their first feedback from the attack as they hooked up with the tankers for their return leg home to Al Udeid – the F-117s had stayed 'cloaked' in silence and had not yet received any information back from base. Once plugged into the tanker, the crew informed them that everything had worked out well. 'How many times in a lifetime does an individual get to take the opening shots designed to liberate a country?' Hoehn reflected. The two pilots had pulled off an incredible mission, and were summarily awarded the Distinguished Flying Cross (DFC) in late April.

ALLIED ATTACKERS

Following the F-117's opening wave of attacks, the 'Shock and Awe' campaign got underway in earnest against Saddam and his Ba'ath Party regime, with incredible scenes beamed around the world. The American, British and Australian assets tackled a wide variety of targets from the outset of the campaign, including key military and regime targets in and around Baghdad and the pounding of Republican Guard positions around the capital.

The Iraqi air defence network called upon SAMs such as the SA-2, SA-3, SA-6, SA-8, SA-9, SA-13 and Roland, as well as triple-A. Most of the radar-guided SAMs were launched 'ballistically', with operators not daring to turn guidance equipment on for the fear of instantaneous SEAD attack from Coalition forces. The area around Baghdad boasted the 'Super Missile Engagement Zone' (Super MEZ) – the Coalition nickname for the maze of SAMs that encircled the city. Missions were soon flown around the clock, with night attacks over Baghdad giving crews a frightening insight into the number of SAMs actually being fired as NVGs clearly highlighted tell-tale streaks into the night sky.

Speaking on 1 April, Maj Gen Stanley A. McChrystal, vice director of operations for the Joint Staff, said that the bombing of Baghdad had been astounding, both in its precision and in its overall effect. 'The pounding that Baghdad has taken has been extraordinarily precise in its nature. It has been nothing like what some people visualise as the destruction of a city. It is focused on regime-oriented targets and very carefully done. Certain things have been pounded, but only those that represent regime targets. Coalition forces have fired more than 700 cruise missiles and have dropped more than 10,000 precision-guided munitions since Operation 'Iraqi Freedom' began'.

At the height of the conflict, Coalition aircraft were flying more than 1,000 sorties a day, focussing on regime leadership targets, Republican Guard divisions and on countering missile threats. Operation 'Iraqi Freedom' also covered an incredible number of 'firsts' from an aerial warfare standpoint (see Appendices section).

Above: **The 1st Fighter Wing F-15Cs from Langley AFB, VA, worked alongside Eagles from Eglin and Kadena to achieve total air supremacy without having to tackle any Iraqi AF fighters. The enemy fighters stayed firmly on the ground throughout the campaign. Before the war started, Iraqi aircraft had tried to lure Coalition patrols into mobile SAM engagement zones.** *Jamie Hunter/aviacom*

Left: **Col Brett Williams prepares for a mission over Iraq in his F-15C. Col Williams was stationed at Prince Sultan AB (PSAB), Saudi Arabia, as part of the 363rd AEW.** *USAF*

EAGLE TALONS

One of the most notable features of the OIF air war was the complete 'no-show' from the Iraqi AF (see also relevant chapter). In 1991's Operation 'Desert Storm' USAF F-15Cs enjoyed rich pickings and stories of aerial victories made headline news. In the build-up to OIF there were stories of Iraqi MiGs trying to lure OSW patrols onto SAM engagement zones, and even reports that a MiG-25 had claimed a USAF UAV and that another had attempted to intercept a U-2 spyplane. However, from the outbreak of hostilities it was clear that Iraq's fighter pilots were staying well and truly on the ground. With USAF F-15Cs, RAF Tornado F3s and RAAF F/A-18A Hornets patrolling the skies under the watchful gaze of E-3 AWACS, air supremacy was quickly established. Three squadrons of F-15Cs were deployed to the region; the 58th FS 'Gorillas' from Eglin

AFB, FL, operated alongside the Langley-based 71st FS 'Ironmen' at Sheikh Isa, Bahrain, while at Prince Sultan AB, Saudi Arabia, the 67th FS 'Fighting Cocks' had already been deployed from Kadena, Japan. The F-15Cs were busy around the clock providing escort and Combat Air Patrols (CAPs), but finding little trade.

As with 'Desert Storm', the 4th FW from Seymour Johnson AFB, NC, featured heavily in OIF, with the wing deploying an impressive 48 F-15E Strike Eagles to Al Udeid AB in Qatar. The 336th FS 'Rocketeers' was joined by the 335th FS 'Chiefs' from late February, with a pooled team of aircrews drawn from Seymour Johnson as well as from the combat-experienced 391st FS 'Bold Tigers' at Mountain Home AFB, ID.

After an initial period of inactivity due to political wrangling in the region, the F-15Es began flying armed Non-Traditional Intelligence Surveillance and Reconnaissance (NTISR) missions over the southern Iraqi No-Fly Zone to collect information on the latest enemy activity. The Strike Eagle crews used their existing LANTIRN (Low Altitude Navigation and Targeting Infra-Red for Night) pods as well as a small number of Northrop Grumman Litening II pods, which had been cleared for use on the Strike Eagle in late 2002, to monitor Iraqi military activity and engage if required. As well as the NTISR missions, the F-15E pilots and WSOs (Weapons System Officers) began practising

Left: **An F-15E Strike Eagle punches out decoy flares as it returns from a mission. The 4th Fighter Wing from Seymour Johnson AFB, SC, deployed 48 F-15Es to the Persian Gulf for OIF.** *Jamie Hunter/aviacom*

Below: **A 4th FW F-15E Strike Eagle receives taxi clearance before it heads out for a mission from Al Udeid AB, Qatar.** *USAF*

Right: **A 4th FW F-15E Strike Eagle armed with GBU-12 laser-guided bombs (LGBs) as well as AIM-120 AMRAAM and AIM-9 Sidewinder missiles, takes on fuel from a USAF KC-10A high above the Iraqi desert.** *Lou Drummond*

the new doctrine of SCAR (Strike Co-ordination Attack and Reconnaissance). This basically involved the F-15E taking control of a 'kill box' to locate, positively identify, evaluate and allocate targets to other strike aircraft in the area, similar to the FAC-A role (Forward Air Control – Airborne) flown by the OA-10 and F-16. The F-15E crews made full use of the 'extra pair of eyes' in the cockpit, with the two-man crew performing particularly well in this role.

As OIF got into full swing, the F-15Es were initially tasked with tackling command, control and communication facilities as well as regime leadership targets with the AGM-130 and GBU-28 Laser-Guided Bombs (LGBs). The SCAR mission practice was also put into effect quickly as the Strike Eagles commenced 'Kill Box Interdiction' missions – employing their own GBU-12 LGBs as well as marshalling other attackers in the kill box. The Strike Eagles also worked closely with Special Forces on the ground in the western Iraqi desert, with the 335th FS spending much of its time operating in this demanding environment.

VIPER VENOM

By far the most numerous USAF fighter type deployed to the region was the Lockheed Martin F-16 Fighting Falcon. Leading the Suppression of Enemy Air Defence (SEAD) push were the F-16CJs, which served to punish hostile Iraqi air defence systems.

The 52nd Fighter Wing from Spangdahlem AB in Germany deployed to the region at short notice and took up a primary role. The 22nd EFS 'Stingers' was the lead unit for the 52nd FW's OIF deployment, with a pool of aircrew boosted by elements of the 23rd FS 'Hawks' deployed together as part of the 379th AEW. The 22nd FS deployed initially with 12 jets to a forward operating base in the Persian Gulf.

Capt Darren Gray, 22nd FS 'Stingers'

'I left for OIF on 10 January to the FOL (Forward Operating Location). I started off flying OSW (Operation 'Southern Watch' – enforcing the Southern Iraqi No-Fly Zone), but it took a while for us to start flying these missions due to clearance. As a result we came up with some ingenious training methods to stay tactically proficient.

'The 22nd FS was airborne on the first day of the war – I was on the night wave. That first night I flew with AGM-88 HARM anti-radiation missiles fitted. We did mostly two-ship formations and, as the VULs (Vulnerability time – periods over enemy territory) were so long, a dedicated package commander would cycle aircraft in and out of the tanker. The first couple of nights we were 'fragged' (tasked) out to join the counter-Scud fight in the west – we were supporting all of the strikers out there. It was a huge challenge trying to provide SEAD support to those guys; they were all over the place trying to find targets of opportunity. We would find them on the radar and try to help them out.

'We have the IDM (Improved Data Modem), so other platforms (such as the Rivet Joint) could datalink us or come

Above: **The USAF deployed 131 Lockheed Martin F-16s for participation in OIF. This AGM-88 HARM-toting F-16CJ is from the 35th FW, 14th FS 'Samurais'.** *USAF*

Below: **The 22nd FS 'Stingers' was the lead unit deployed from Spangdahlem AB, Germany. Capt Darren Gray is the squadron weapons officer and is seen here strapping in for a mission in his F-16CJ. Note the aircraft carries JDAM and HARM mission marks. Spangdahlem gained JDAM capability shortly before deployment.** *Jamie Hunter/aviacom*

up on voice and either pass us co-ordinates or tell us about sites that may be coming up. Primarily though, we were autonomous and worked with our own sensors. Once we get the Sniper pod (the USAF's next-generation advanced targeting pod), we're going to be able to find, identify and kill targets with even more proficiency. Overall our missions were pretty diverse. During my missions, I fired two HARMs and dropped a bunch of JDAMs (Joint Direct Attack Munitions) and CBU-103 WCMDs (Wind Corrected Munitions Dispensers). Some of these were for CAS (Close Air Support) missions whilst others were for TST (Time Sensitive Targeting). I also undertook one DEAD (Destruction of Enemy Air Defence) mission against an SA-2 site.

'As we mainly flew at night, we were flying on NVGs (Night Vision Goggles), but in the role we undertook most guys

turned the NVGs off. All the JDAM and WCMD worked like a charm. As for the HARM, I could see them impact but it's tough for BDA (Battle Damage Assessment). When I dropped the JDAM, I knew it hit because I saw the secondary explosion go off.

'Amazingly enough, one of the things that surprised me the most about this war was that we saw more missiles and AAA than I could count – but none of it was guided – and they never turned their radars on. On that first night I thought, for sure, we were going to be coming home having expended our HARMs but we were so effective just by being there – they didn't even turn the systems on. The two HARM shots I took were actually a pre-emptive launch for the support of other assets.

'I also supported the US Navy F-14s and F/A-18s, as well as the US Marines in the East and the Army in the western desert.

'The F-16CJ mission is expanding and it's a huge challenge. In fact, there's never a dull moment as the squadron Weapons Officer – we are constantly upgrading, coming up with new tactics and new ways to do business. When fully operational, the Link-16 datalink system is going to give us huge SA (Situational Awareness) not only on 'red' players but also 'blues'. Also, once we get the Sniper system, the AGM-65 Maverick is going to be a huge asset. You can find the site, ID it with the Sniper pod and correlate it with the Maverick, then fire and leave'.

Capt Bradley 'Boomer' Roth, 23rd FS 'Hawks'

'I got there as part of the first group of 23rd FS personnel in the beginning of February. I started to fly straight away. After a week we began OSW and we continued these (mainly SEAD) missions right up until the start of OIF.

'Iraq was divided up into lanes and we would operate as SEAD support for a large area. We would roam around in the darkness as all missions were at night. The first few nights we had a few four-ship packages, but the majority of the sorties were two-ship.

'In those first nights, we flew in support of strike packages going over Baghdad. We didn't know what to expect and saw some ballistically-launched SAMs, all unguided. When you see AAA and missiles it really concentrates the mind.

'The first week we were part of an overall package, after that it was pretty much a case of having three two-ship packages airborne at any one time, roaming around and being responsible for an area between Tikrit and Najaf. They'd be co-ordinated with each other and while one pair was on the tanker, the others would be taking care of each other. The strikers would then come in and whoever was the SEAD at the time would cover them. We were averaging 8-9hr missions. We had about an hour's transit to the tanker, which started out over Saudi and then pushed up towards Baghdad. We would then execute three 45min 'VUL time' periods over enemy territory.

Left: **On the EOR (End Of Runway) at Al Udeid, F-16CJs of the 22nd EFS 'Stingers' flew missions alongside the 157th EFS 'Swamp Foxes'.** *USAF*

Below: **The 20th FW's F-16CJs from Shaw AFB, SC, played a vital role on the opening nights in OIF. The F-16CJ is the USAF's primary Suppression of Enemy Air Defence (SEAD) strike platform.** *USAF*

'The jet was excellent – you could say we were over qualified. The Iraqi air-defence system was almost non-existent. A lot of the air strikes had taken out the crucial air-defence nodes that were making the Iraqi SAM sites autonomous, which meant they weren't doing very well.

'I shot two HARMs and also dropped some JDAM and WCMD. JDAM performed great. It's very easy to use and the feedback was usually 'direct hit'. We mainly programmed the bomb in-flight as we were doing Time Sensitive Targeting – we never really took off with a pre-determined strike mission. For SEAD we did a bit of both pre-planned and in-flight targeting. Also, the F-16 guys from Shaw AFB did a lot of strafing as they were flying daytime missions.

'The FACs we worked with were mostly US Marines, USAF and US Army. We were given the co-ordinates and just typed that into the computer. All the PID (Positive Identification) and collateral and assessment was done by the FAC.

'We used IDM to check that all the aircraft had the same co-ordinates – we could share this data on our cockpit screens. Another bonus of this system is that, if you momentarily lose visual, then the IDM can help you get back together.

'In terms of the Viper's future war employment, the F-16's CCIP (Common Configuration Implementation Program) upgrade will help with our overall SA, especially once we get Link-16 as we'll be able to see what everybody else is seeing – it will take a lot of the radio talk out of the loop. The JHMCS (Joint Helmet Mounted Cueing System) will enable us to look at something on the ground and designate it, but it's the Sniper pod that will be the biggest thing for us for any future combat'.

Capt TC 'Beef' Curry, 23rd FS 'Hawks'

'I got out there in early March. A week later the war kicked off and I started flying. There weren't as many threats as we had expected. I flew all my missions at night, yet I'd only had 5hrs on NVGs before the war – a testament to the Viper as a great platform.

'I think everybody flew a CAS mission of some sort. It got to the point where we had such good intel and less of a threat that they could call us in and pretty much talk us onto the target. Our attacks were very strictly controlled. If there was any doubt, we didn't drop our bombs.

'Until this, I didn't know what it was like to have a missile shot at you. Every missile I saw, I thought it was flying at me, but after a couple of flights I was able to recognise if a missile was aimed at me or not. The longest mission I flew lasted 8.5hrs and I went to the tanker four times in that period. Overall, I felt like the war was a lot more organised than I ever expected it to be and a lot more restricted. If you didn't know what you were going to drop on – you didn't drop'.

New technology

Maj Adrian 'Kermit' Pone led the introduction of the all-important Joint Direct Attack Munition (JDAM) for the 52nd FW prior to deploying for OIF.

'JDAM was used by F-16 squadrons in OEF (Operation 'Enduring Freedom') so we were not the first Block 50s to use the weapon. The 169th FW South Carolina ANG and 389th FS, 366th Wing guys at Mountain Home have also used JDAM, but OIF was the first time that the Spangdahlem Block 50 jets had employed it.

Below: **A package of Spangdahlem-based Block 50 F-16CJs from the 22nd EFS 'Stingers' and 23rd EFS 'Hawks' heads out from the unit's forward operating base for a SEAD mission over Iraq. These F-16s carry both AGM-88 HARMs and GPS-guided GBU-31 JDAMs.** *USAF*

Inset: **A female pilot (callsign 'Vixen') from the 157th EFS 'Swamp Foxes', South Carolina ANG, prepares to launch into the night from Al Udeid, Qatar, for a SEAD mission.** *USAF*

'In OIF, JDAM quickly became one of the most commonly used weapons – particularly towards the end. Obviously it's an all-weather munition, you don't have to support it with a laser and it's really simple to use. You just make sure it's powered up and it's linking with satellites and you let it go. You can drop it at pretty far ranges, depending on how fast and high you are.

'We don't have a targeting pod on the CJ variant of the F-16 yet, but all you really need in the case of JDAM is a good set of co-ordinates for the target. We would normally get these co-ordinates from third party source who would send them to the cockpit via IDM, but we'd usually get them via the radio.

'We were carrying AGM-88 HARM anti-radiation missiles on our initial missions. However, the ground force's push northwards happened in days and, with such a vast area of land occupied very quickly, there wasn't such a concern over the SAM threat. For that reason less emphasis was placed on shooting HARMs and more on dropping bombs. As a result, we took the HARMs off and a typical two-ship package ended up carrying either JDAM or WCMD.

'Although we have JSOW (Joint-Stand Off Weapon) flight cleared on the F-16, we didn't use it in OIF. It is not a commonly used weapon at the moment. It has got a much better stand-off capability than JDAM so in a higher threat scenario we could have employed it. We just didn't need to.

'Elsewhere in the Viper's repertoire, the Sniper pod will represent a quantum leap in our capabilities when the system receives full operational clearance. I've seen the difference between LANTIRN and Litening and there's a pretty big jump, but Sniper will be huge. To help train for the new mission we're getting new simulators in Spring 2004.

'Also, the CCIP (Common Configuration Implementation Program) software improvements further down the road will give us increased capabilities over the battlefield, particularly with the introduction of the Link-16 datalink system'. The first 52nd FW jets went in for upgrade to CCIP standard before OIF kicked off. This fleet-wide modernisation is designed to introdcuce a host of latest common capabilities to the F-16 and will further improve the 52nd FW's warfighting flexibility.

Shaw shots

As OIF got underway two squadrons from the 20th FW at Shaw AFB, SC, were representative of a Stateside-based unit sent to the region. The 55th FS was deployed to Incirlik AB, Turkey, to fly Operation 'Northern Watch' patrols over Iraq while the 77th FS 'Gamblers' deployed to Azraq, Jordan, as part of the 410th AEW.

As it became clear that Turkey had resisted pressure to use its bases for a northern front on Iraq, the 55th FS was effectively grounded with no opportunity to participate in OIF. However, under the leadership of Lt Col Jon Norman, the 'Gamblers' were busy flying SEAD and CAS missions from the outset. One notable mission saw the squadron being called-in to 'take out' a downed US Army AH-64D shortly after it appeared in a regional TV broadcast. A laser-guided bomb dropped by F-16CJ 91-0348 ensured the Iraqis were unable to exploit the helicopter's technology (see also War Paint appendix).

As the squadron moved from SEAD to FAC-A and CAS missions, the only damage they suffered was minor self-inflicted wounds. Several aircraft from the 77th had 20mm cannon shells explode as they exited the barrel of the gun, puncturing the aircraft skin. One pilot recounted; 'I had no idea

that I had a problem until the crew chief pointed to the nose as I returned to base'.

The CAS aspect of the campaign was particularly important as the ground force progressed towards Baghdad. As the ground threats diminished, commanders were keen to emphasise safety concerns. Lt Col Grant Bishop, an F-16CJ pilot commented at the time 'It may look like things are slowing down, but there are coalition fighters in the air 24 hours a day around Iraq making sure no problems exist'.

Above: **A quartet of South Carolina ANG Block 52 F-16CJs adorned with OIF mission marks pose for the camera. The Block 52 F-16 is powered by the Pratt & Whitney F100-PW-229 engine, unlike the Block 50 that features the General Electric F110-GE-129.** *Greg L. Davis*

Swamp Foxes

Another significant F-16CJ deployment was the 169th Fighter Wing, 157th Expeditionary Fighter Squadron 'Swamp Foxes' of the South Carolina ANG, which deployed to Al Udeid in February 2003. The unit deployed 13 of its F-16CJs and two F-16CJs loaned from the 389th FS at Mountain Home AFB. The additional jets were drafted in to the SC ANG contingent because it had two of its own aircraft undergoing the CCIP upgrade.

The 'Swamp Foxes' worked closely with other F-16 units to provide SEAD missions for the Coalition. The 157th EFS flew 411 combat sorties, notching up a total of 2,322 combat hours. As well as SEAD missions (with AGM-88 HARMs), the unit also flew CAS missions (dropping JDAMs, WCMDs, GBU-12 Laser-Guided Bombs) and even the 20mm cannon.

According to the 169th Operations Group Commander, Lt Col Deane D. Pennington, the 'Swamp Foxes' became the first and only F-16CJ unit to drop laser-guided bombs with the LANTIRN and Litening II targeting pod. The Litening II pods were only available in limited numbers in the ANG/AFRC inventory at the start of OIF. To make matters worse, those pods were spread out across the various communities to allow units to train with the popular new kit. So, rather than having to deploy with insufficient equipment, the SC ANG utilised its C-130H Hercules transport to make a dash across the various bases to pick-up every available pod for immediate deployment.

HOG HAVEN

Operation 'Desert Storm' marked a rejuvenation in the fortunes of the Fairchild Republic A-10A Thunderbolt II – the tank-busting attributes of the 'Hog' came to the fore as it smashed Iraqi armour. For Operation 'Iraqi Freedom' the robust type was again to show its worth with the USAF deploying 60 A/OA-10s in the build-up to the conflict.

The A-10 has been largely overlooked when it comes to upgrades, however, the need for target marking was realised in the months before OIF when the Thunderbolt IIs of the 118th FS Connecticut ANG and 104th FS Massachusetts ANG received the ability to carry the Litening II targeting pod.

During OIF, each A-10 pilot routinely flew a mission a day. As of 22 April, the A-10 force had flown more than 3,100 sorties hunting down the Iraqi Republican Guard, looking for Scud sites in western Iraq and providing CAS for ground forces.

While flying one such mission over Baghdad on 7 April, Capt Kim Campbell of the 23rd FG from Pope AFB, NC, was hit by anti-aircraft fire as she supported ground troops. With her aircraft's warning lights flashing and it having lost both hydraulic systems, Capt Campbell was unable to control the A-10 as it banked sharply to the left and nosed downward. But the A-10 is built for survival. The titanium-armoured 'bathtub' cockpit and redundant flight control systems give it an incredible 'get home' capability after being hit. 'We were taking fire almost the entire time we were in the area, when I heard a loud bang and felt the initial impact', Campbell said. After several attempts to get the jet under control, Campbell switched to manual control and found she could still fly the crippled aircraft. Capt Campbell's flight lead, Lt Col Richard Turner, monitored the situation; 'The jet was flying pretty well, and the damage had not affected the flight control surfaces or the landing gear. If she could keep it flying, we would get out of Baghdad and might be able to

Left: A line up of Air Force Reserve Command (AFRC) A/OA-10As from the 442nd FW at Whiteman AFM, MO, at Tallil AB in Iraq. As troops pushed north the A-10s were able to provide support at short notice thanks to the use this base inside enemy territory. *USAF*

Below: The 'Hogs' of the 190th FS, Idaho ANG, were amongst the first aircraft to occupy the ex-Iraqi AF base at Tallil to form the 392nd AEW. This example carries a mixed load of Mk82 iron bombs, an AGM-65 Maverick and an LAU-7 white-phosphorus target marker rocket pod. *USAF*

make it back to base'. Having coaxed the ailing 'Hog' for a further hour, Capt Campbell managed to make it back to her forward operating base. 'The jet worked perfectly, which is a tribute to our maintainers and the guys who work on the jet. It's nice when things work as advertised' she commented.

As the frontline moved north towards Baghdad, a number of Iraqi facilities were captured and secured to become forward operating bases. Lt Gerardo Gonzalez is a public affairs officer with the 52nd FW at Spangdahlem AB, Germany. He deployed to Tallil in Iraq for 60 days with the 407th Air Expeditionary Group. 'It was just a big, dusty, hot base' he recalled. The A-10As of the 'Flying Tigers' at Pope AFB, NC, were stationed at Tallil to fly CAS missions, along with USAF RQ-1 Predators and Special Ops HC-130s. The move into Tallil allowed the A-10s to spend more time over the battlefield and rapidly react to emerging threats.

Above left: **A USAF A-10A Thunderbolt II screams in towards its target in the Iraqi desert. The strafing of hapless enemy positions with the devastating 30mm GAU8/A Avenger seven-barrelled Gatling cannon was, once again, extremely effective.** *USAF*

Left: **Tankbuster's lair. An A-10A Thunderbolt II deployed from Pope AFB taxies past a derelict Iraqi tank at Tallil.** *USAF Lt Gonzalez*

Below: **Mean machine. This battle scarred 23rd FG A-10A is inspected at Al Jaber AB, Kuwait, after returning from another mission in the heat of the action.** *USAF*

HEAVY METAL

Rapid establishment of air supremacy (or even air dominance), coupled with precision weapons and the ability to quickly locate and attack targets gave the Coalition an impressive foothold from the outset of OIF. The USAF bomber fleet attacked targets ranging from strategic sites, such as those struck on 'night one', to individual tanks and artillery pieces throughout Iraq. The plan was simple – to degrade and ultimately destroy the ability of the Ba'ath Party regime to exercise command and control of the Iraqi military. Throughout the campaign it became increasingly evident that all of Iraq's military forces, including regular Army units, those of the Republican Guard and the remains of its Integrated Air Defence System (IADS) were quickly resigned to total paralysis.

The USAF's heavy bomber force went on to showcase its unique capabilities once again, with its assets undertaking some incredibly complex missions. While many of the missions flown in the first days of the campaign were planned and flown against pre-assigned target sets, USAF bomber sorties soon changed to an 'on call' capability. For example, the Rockwell

Left: **Clutching an impressive load of CBU-105 WCMDs, a B-52H of the USAF's 5th BW takes off from RAF Fairford, UK, for the long mission down to Iraq. Operation 'Iraqi Freedom' marked the first use of this precision weapon by the 'BUFF'.** *Richard Cooper*

Left: As night falls, the B-2A stealth bomber comes into its own to deliver a silent and deadly strike. The Spirits operated from Whiteman AFB, MO, as well as Diego Garcia in the Indian Ocean. *USAF*

Above: Having missed out on Operation 'Desert Storm', the USAF's B-1B Lancer fleet has truly made its mark during subsequent operations. During OIF B-1s operated from Thumrait, Oman, and were able to react to Time Sensitive Targets (TSTs). *Jamie Hunter/aviacom*

Below: Operation 'Iraqi Freedom' marked the first time the USAF has flown a mission involving B-2A Spirits, B-1B Lancers and B-52H Stratofortresses as a joint strike package. *USAF*

B-1B Lancers and Boeing B-52H Stratofortresses launched with a set of notional targets as well as an assigned orbit area and 'VUL time' to cover. The USAF's Northrop Grumman B-2A Spirit stealth bomber fleet was also heavily involved from the start, striking high-value targets in the most hostile of environments – most notably in and around Baghdad.

The combat phase of the air campaign saw a number of notable firsts, especially within this potent heavy bomber community. Lt Col Kevin Anderson, Chief Master Air Attack Plan, described how the USAF flew a unique joint B-1B, B-2A and B-52H package. 'For the first time, we have used all three bombers in one package at the same time. All the bombers used GPS-aimed weapons to generate a devastating attack on a single target window. As well as allowing us to put a lot of weapons on the target at the same time, there is also the psychological effect of having all three bombers over a target at once'.

For the first time, a female pilot flew combat missions in the B-2 Spirit. Capt Jennifer Wilson was deployed to Diego Garcia with the 393rd Expeditionary Bomb Squadron (EBS), having arrived in theatre from Whiteman AFB, MO, on 1 April. She commented; 'Flying is great. I can't imagine doing anything else

right now, and to be able to have a chance to fly in combat with the B-2 was an awesome experience'.

A former B-1 Lancer pilot, Capt Wilson had previously flown combat missions during Operation 'Allied Force' over Kosovo. 'I wasn't scared. We've all trained quite a bit leading up to this operation. I knew I was going to be able to come through and get the job done'. The global reach achieved by USAF bombers was well illustrated during OIF, with sorties originating from as far away as Whiteman AFB, MO; RAF Fairford, Gloucestershire, UK; Diego Garcia in the Indian Ocean and Thumrait in Oman. The longest of these missions was undertaken by a Whiteman-based B-2A, which flew a mind-numbing 34hr round trip.

'BUFF' attack

The USAF B-52H force is in constant demand around the globe due to its awesome capabilities and fearsome reputation.

The mighty 'BUFF' has repeatedly proved itself as a highly potent asset; nothing can be more demoralising for an enemy force than the sight of the deadly bomber circling high overhead. In the build-up to OIF, B-52s from the 5th BW at Minot AFB, ND, deployed to RAF Fairford, UK, under the 457th AEG and aircraft from the 2nd BW at Barksdale, LA, headed for Diego Garcia in the Indian Ocean to form the 40th AEW. As well as the 28 B-52Hs initially deployed for OIF, around 10 2nd BW aircraft were sent to Guam as a show of force towards the actions of North Korea.

Below: **With the famous smokey trails streaming from the water-injected TF33 engines, a Minot-based B-52H attached to the 457th AEG at RAF Fairford, UK, lumbers into the air on its way to Iraq. Some 120 combat sorties were flown from RAF Fairford.** *Richard Cooper*

Above: A sinister Northrop Grumman B-2A Spirit is seen dropping back from a KC-135R having received fuel on a Global Power combat mission from Whiteman AFB, MO, the longest of which lasted an amazing 34 hours. *USAF*

Below: Far into enemy territory, a B-52H pilot assigned to the 40th EBS prepares for action. At this point the crew will be in touch with ground forces receiving updated battlefield information. The introduction of the Litening II pod allowed the 'BUFF' to autonomously identify and attack targets. Ground co-ordinates supplied by Ground Forward Air Controllers (GFACs) also allowed the B-52 to employ the JDAM and WCMD GPS-guided munitions with devastating effect against Iraqi military positions. *USAF*

As 'Shock and Awe' got underway, the B-52s were playing a key role. The 40th EBS commenced its contribution on 21 March when 10 B-52s crewed by both Active Duty and Reserve crewmembers headed out with a total of 76 internally mounted AGM-86 Conventional Air Launched Cruise Missiles (CALCM). Several of the aircraft were also loaded with 12 external GBU-31 2,000lb JDAMs.

From the outset, the Diego Garcia-based 40th EBS hit Iraqi control and communication sites, Republican Guard positions, airfields, armour, artillery, tanks and vehicles. En-route to Iraq, bomber crews contacted command and control assets and received updated taskings. These 'flex' assignments ranged

from strategic targets such as leadership or command, control, communications and intelligence facilities to direct support of ground forces, sometimes working with Ground-based Forward Air Controllers (GFACs). A GFAC would typically pass target details to the bombers and clear them in for the attack. It was evident that the JDAM had become the weapon of choice when working with GFACs to knock out Iraqi armour.

Building on its already combat-proven past, the 'BUFF' was also to herald a new range of capabilities during OIF. On 2 April, B-52s dropped six sensor-fused cluster bombs on a column of Iraqi tanks heading south out of Baghdad. The bombing runs resulted in the destruction of the tanks and marked the first time in history that the CBU-105 WCMDs had been used in combat. The CBU-105 is a deadly GPS-guided precision cluster-bomb that disperses 'bomblets', which can even sense engine heat from armoured vehicles and fire downward to deliver a devastating blow. The weapon's 'wind-compensating' technology effectively steers the bomb to its target – taking adverse conditions into consideration to ensure maximum punch right where it's needed.

Above: **Carrying an impressive external load of GBU-31 Joint Direct Attack Munitions (JDAMs), a B-52H heads for its target. Able to loiter and react with precision accuracy, the B-52 is the ultimate airpower asset, able to strike terror into the heart of the enemy.** *USAF*

Above right: **High above the thick cloud, a 405th EBS B-1B noses into the tanker for fuel. The B-1's arsenal of GPS-guided weapons allows the aircraft to 'bomb through' even the poorest weather.** *USAF*

As well as the regular air force units, the US Air National Guard (ANG) and Air Force Reserve Command (AFRC) all made key contributions to the Coalition assault on Iraq. The AFRC deployed three B-52Hs from the 917th Wing, 93rd BS to RAF Fairford in early April in order to begin operations with the newly integrated Litening II targeting pod. The Litening pod greatly increased the aircrew's options over the battlefield, ideal for a loitering B-52. The crew could now independently identify and designate targets to better serve forces on the ground and meet the ever-changing demands of the conflict.

For B-52s flying long-range missions from bases such as Fairford, arriving over the target area several hours after take-

off meant that the crew had to be able to respond to changes and new requirements. Pre-programmed GPS weapons are only as good as the co-ordinates supplied, so if a target had moved, Litening would allow a suitably equipped B-52H to react accordingly.

The first long-range Litening mission from Fairford struck targets at an airfield in northern Iraq on 11 April and was reported as being a complete success. A Litening-equipped B-52H with a mixed crew from the 93rd BS from Barksdale and the 23rd BS at Minot had dropped a laser-guided GBU-12 on a radar complex and another on a command complex at the airfield.

Commenting on the success of the Litening integration on the B-52, Brig Gen Jack Ihle, commander of the 917th Wing, said 'We're very excited about the B-52 Litening II targeting pod program and the enhanced capabilities the pod will provide. The Litening II pod is a self-contained, multi-sensor laser target designating and navigation system. It allows the crew to detect, acquire, track and identify ground targets independently for highly accurate delivery of weapons, both conventional and laser-guided, from well above 30,000ft'.

The B-52s typically carried either 12 JDAMs or 16 CBU-105 WCMDs externally, along with general-purpose (GP) bombs in the internal bay. The 'BUFF' went on to drop a total of 300 JDAMs, 157 M117s, around 1,000 Mk82s and fired 80 AGM-86s during OIF.

By 19 April the 40th EBS operating from Diego Garcia had flown 137 combat sorties with 2,157.5hrs of flight time, while the Fairford-based 457th AEG had accrued 120 combat missions.

By the end of the air combat phase of the campaign, the 40th EBS had delivered over 3,300 weapons to include CALCM, JDAM, CBU-103/105 WCMD, Mk117, Mk82, Mk84 and Mk129 – a massive combined total of close to 3,000,000lb of

ordnance. The overall figures for OIF had become equally impressive; by 23 April 2003 CENTCOM reported total sorties since 19 March were around 47,600, with strike sorties put at 17,200.

Bad to the B-One

The USAF deployed 11 Rockwell B-1B Lancers (a type commonly referred to as 'Bone') to Thumrait, Oman, as part of the 405th AEW. The weapons loadout for the menacing B-1 was usually a mix of conventional warhead and penetration versions of the GBU-31 JDAM, with eight weapons loaded in each of the Lancer's three bomb bays.

One of the most well documented missions of the entire campaign was the attack on a suspected meeting of Saddam Hussein and his sons by a 34th EBS B-1B Lancer (86-0138, *Seek and Destroy*) from Thumrait on 7 April. The strike on the Al Mansour district of Baghdad saw Capt Chris Wachter, Capt Sloan Hollis and WSOs Lt Col Fred Swan and 1st Lt Joe Runci deliver four GBU-31 JDAMs within minutes of receiving the target details.

Lt Col Swan detailed 'We were just coming off the tanker in western Iraq with another target area we were planning to go to, and we were re-tasked to this target. From the time we got the co-ordinates it took 12 minutes to get the bombs on target'. This was a good illustration of how the US military has dramatically narrowed the 'sensor to shooter' gap, with reports suggesting that it took just one hour from intelligence identifying the target to the B-1 delivering its deadly payload.

Once the highly time-sensitive target had been identified, the airborne B-1 was passed new target co-ordinates by an E-3 Sentry, with the crew then re-programming four JDAMs with

Right: **A B-1B of the 28th Bomb Wing deployed to Thumrait, Oman, from its home base at Ellsworth AFB, SD.** *USAF*

the new target details. Of the four GBU-31 JDAMs dropped in the attack, the first two had 'hard-penetration' capability with delayed fusing, followed by two standard versions. This bomb mix was chosen 'to achieve the desired effect of destroying the building while minimising collateral damage'. With its target area completely devastated, the B-1 went on to two further locations about 200 miles away and attack a further 17 targets.

The B-1s were also kept very busy supporting ground forces forging north towards Baghdad. Lancers from the 405th Air Expeditionary Wing at Thumrait came under heavy enemy fire during their first few combat missions. According to Capt Ty Newman, a B-1 WSO, 'The threat is certainly out there, and on any given mission we take every precaution and use all our tactics to minimise the threat to our aircraft as we go on strikes inside Baghdad'.

In a final summary of the 'Bone's' successful campaign, the vice-Commander of the 405th AEW Col Peter Kippie stated 'There wasn't a target within Iraq that was not at risk when we took off'. The B-1 has evolved into a potent precision striker.

WATCHING THE ENEMY

It is acknowledged that the US military has unparalleled intelligence gathering capabilities. It is able to draw on an immense range of platforms and systems to create an incredibly detailed 'picture' of the battlespace. Intelligence, Surveillance and Reconnaissance (ISR) assets deployed for OIF by the USAF, US Navy and the RAF gave commanders total insight into the unfolding battle through Electronic Intelligence (ELINT), Signal Intelligence (SIGINT) and Imagery Intelligence (IMINT), with the data collected by manned, unmanned and satellite platforms.

One of the greatest airpower triumphs of Operation 'Iraqi Freedom' was the employment of the Northrop Grumman E-8 J-STARS (Joint Surveillance Target Attack Radar System, installed in a Boeing 707 airframe). This highly prized asset provides an up-to-the-minute relay of enemy ground movements and was vital to the campaign. The E-8s flew 193

combat missions and were airborne for 3,099hrs during the combat phase of OIF, with some missions lasting up to 23hrs. USAF Chief of Staff, Gen John P. Jumper described the E-8's performance as 'a resounding success'. The blended ANG and active USAF 116th Air Control Wing (ACW) from Robins AFB, GA, deployed with nine E-8C J-STARS. These aircraft employ a Moving Target Indicator (MTI) radar to precisely track ground enemy ground movements, which can then be handed over to be identified by reconnaissance platforms with Synthetic Aperture Radar (SAR) or Electro-Optical (EO) sensors. This

Below: **The Northrop Grumman E-8C J-STARS proved highly effective during OIF. The aircraft employs a Moving Target Indicator (MTI) radar to precisely track ground enemy ground movements. This example is seen transiting through RAF Mildenhall on its way back from the campaign.** *Peter J. Cooper/Falcon Aviation*

allowed Coalition commanders to react to emerging threats such as counter attacks and convoys. Attack aircraft were able to then 'go in' and PID the target before engaging.

The E-8s enabled ground forces to receive the latest 'ground picture' of the battlefield, even in the appalling sandstorms that hit a few days into the war. Indeed, it was during these storms that the Iraqi Army mounted a counter attack on an element of the US Army 3-7th Cavalry, 3rd Infantry Division, near Najaf. A patrolling J-STARS alerted the ground force and an immediate strike thwarted the Iraqi offensive.

One particular new capability put into action was the ability for the E-8 to datalink MTI target information directly to the cockpit of the US Army AH-64D Longbow Apache attack helicopter. Indeed, the US Army, along with the US Marine Corps, praised the capabilities and effect of working so closely with the J-STARS.

The ability to manage and shape the battlespace is one of the true strengths of the US military. The USAF has excellent ISR assets and, operating alongside the J-STARS, the 55th Wing's RC-135V/W Rivet Joint SIGINT platform is another vital link in the information chain for commanders. Nine 'RJs' deployed to Prince Sultan AB in Saudi Arabia and to Souda Bay, Crete, for OIF. An RC-135 was 'on station' throughout the war, high above Iraq, watching and listening to the unfolding conflict. The aircraft is a sponge for electronic activity, soaking up intelligence to be monitored and interpreted by the crew. It is able to track and identify a multitude of systems from hostile radars (to help the SEAD forces), to enemy communications – even mobile phone conversations. The Rivet Joints worked with AWACS, EC-130H Compass Calls, UAVs, and strike platforms to severely hamper the Iraqi defences. The 'no-show' of the Iraqi air defence network has been largely attributed to the skills of the RC-135 and its crews.

Well known for its battlefield management attributes, the E-3 AWACS worked closely with the J-STARS and the Rivet Joint throughout OIF to direct strike aircraft to emerging threats and keep commanders in touch with the latest developments with the 'air picture'. The USAF and the RAF had deployed a combined total of 19 of these airborne radar platforms as the ultimate 'eyes' over the battlespace. The AWACS team is kept constantly busy directing fighters with taskings, co-ordinating packages of aircraft, de-conflicting air traffic and alerting 'friendlies' of threats – it is a vital asset.

On the reconnaissance side, the 9th RW fielded its new combined team of Lockheed Martin U-2Ss and RQ-4A Global Hawks for OIF. An incredible total of 15 U-2s were deployed

Left: **Having topped up its tanks from a KC-10, a USAF E-3 AWACS heads back 'on task' over Iraq. The AWACS is the 'eyes' over the battlefield and gives commanders an up-to-date 'air picture' around the clock.** *USAF*

Below: **Touching down at Souda Bay, Crete, this 95th RS RC-135W is fitted with the new CFM-56-F108 engines being introduced across the fleet. Souda Bay was home to the 398th Air Expeditionary Wing during OIF.** *USAF*

Above: A U-2S seen getting airborne for a reconnaissance mission from Prince Sultan AB (PSAB) during OIF. The aircraft features the ASARS-2 nose as well as wing sensor 'superpods'. The starboard wing's 'Senior Ruby' pod is fitted with the COMINT (Communications Intelligence) antennas underneath. The pod on the port side is also 'Senior Ruby' but fitted with the 'Senior Spear' COMINT fairing underneath. Behind the tailwheel the spherical piece of equipment is the datalink. This downlinks information to the deployed MOBSTR (Mobile Stretch) ground station, which was in Kuwait for OIF. This then relays data back to Beale AFB, CA; Langley, VA; or the region's CAOC. The U-2's ASARS-2 sensor now has both Synthetic Aperture Radar (SAR) and Moving Target Indicator (MTI) modes. *USAF*

Left: Wearing the full high-altitude pressure suit, Lt Col Walter Flint prepares for a mission over Iraq in his Lockheed Martin U-2S. *USAF*

Below: The 9th RW's U-2S 'Dragonlady' fleet can be configured with various sensor fits to best suit a diversity of reconnaissance missions. This example, attached to the 363rd AEW at PSAB, features the ASARS-2 (Advanced Synthetic Aperture Radar System-2) nose as well as 'Senior Ruby' flat-sided SIGINT (Signals Intelligence) wing 'superpods'. *USAF*

from Beale AFB, CA, for 'Iraqi Freedom' and little about their involvement has been documented except for the launch of six U-2s to support a single Air Tasking Order (ATO) during the war. The Global Hawks proved extremely versatile utilising onboard Synthetic Aperture Radar (SAR), electro-optical (EO) and Infra-Red (IR) sensors to gather information. The long-endurance, high-altitude UAVs reportedly identified over 300 Iraqi tanks as well as numerous SAM sites and they also played key roles in the first combat Strike Co-ordination Attack and Reconnaissance (SCAR) missions of OIF – tackling Iraqi ground forces in tandem with strike platforms. This important collaboration between manned and unmanned aerial assets over a live battlefield marked a huge technological milestone – the significance of which cannot be understated.

Silent killers

The USAF deployed both the RQ-1L reconnaissance and MQ-1L multi-mission variant of the Predator Unmanned Aerial Vehicle (UAV) over Iraq during the campaign. Assets from both the 11th and 15th Reconnaissance Squadrons (RS) deployed to the Persian Gulf and were assigned to the 380th and 386th AEWs.

The RQ-1L is equipped specifically to provide real-time imagery but is also capable of being used to designate targets for laser-guided weapon attack by attack aircraft. For these missions the RQ-1 is equipped with the AN/AAS-53 multi-spectral targeting system (MTS) with electro-optical and infrared (EO/IR) sensors and an integral laser designator. The

Top: **One of the real surprise deployments for OIF was Boeing NKC-135E 'Big Crow' (serial 53-3132) seen here passing through RAF Mildenhall in March 2003. The aircraft was designed to create a hostile electronic warfare (EW) environment and features multiple active EW antennas in large dorsal and ventral radomes and is used for electronic jamming purposes. 'Big Crow' returned to the US on 26 April 2003 having completed 19 OIF-related missions.** *Peter R. Foster*

Centre left: **The Boeing RC-135S 'Cobra Ball' is a ballistic missile signature and telemetry collection platform. The aircraft's OIF duty may well have been to track any potential missile launches by the Iraqi military. On return to its home base at Offutt, NE, in April, the aircraft had received the name *Camel Ballz* and a number of mission marks had been applied.** *Daniel Beedon*

Centre right: **According to USAF figures, as many as seven EC-130H 'Compass Call' electronic warfare Hercules deployed from their home base at Davis-Monthan AFB, AZ, for OIF. These aircraft reportedly flew a total of 125 jamming and psychological warfare missions of up to eight hours each. It was the first combat use of the 'Compass Call' for 'psyops' duties, with the aircraft sharing this mission with an EC-130E 'Commando Solo II'.** *Jamie Hunter/aviacom*

RQ-1 is also capable of carrying the Northrop Grumman AN/ZPQ-1 tactical endurance synthetic aperture radar (TESAR). The EO/IR television cameras and radar allow the aircraft to 'see' through smoke, haze and clouds and provide the information to field commanders in 'real time'. The Predator is also equipped with a line-of-sight (LOS) datalink that allows it to be controlled at ranges of up to 150nm (278km) by a pilot in

Right: The RQ-1 UAV is able to carry the Northrop Grumman AN/ZPQ-1 tactical endurance synthetic aperture radar (TESAR). The EO/IR television cameras and radar allow the aircraft to 'see' through smoke, haze and clouds and provide the information to field commanders in real-time. *USAF Lt Gonzalez*

Below right: Armed and dangerous. A 15th ERS MQ-1L UAV prepares for a mission, armed with a single AGM-114 Hellfire missile. *USAF*

Bottom: Seen at the captured Iraqi base at Tallil, a 64th Expeditionary Reconnaissance Squadron (ERS) Predator Unmanned Aerial Vehicle (UAV) returns to its hangar after a night mission behind enemy lines. *USAF*

the Ground Control Station (GCS) while a second crewmember serves as the sensor operator and controls the cameras and radar. Satellite communications can also be used to permit extended-range operations.

The MQ-1L is equipped with a pair of wing-mounted pylons for carrying the devastating Hellfire II missile, and operates very much as a hunter/killer. As well as being piloted remotely from the GCS, reports during the war indicated that control stations had been added to a number of USAF AC-130 gunships.

As the Predator entered the campaign, it quickly stamped its mark on the war. An MQ-1 found and destroyed a radar-guided anti-aircraft station near Al Amarah in southern Iraq on 22 March, making it the first Predator strike of the operation. Predator pilot Capt Traz Trzaskoma gave details of their valuable work 'Information is gathered around the clock. We immediately pass on any data we gather to the people on the ground who need it. We've been watching for where the bad guys hide, move or want to hide and, if we're carrying Hellfire missiles, we can take care of a target ourselves. In one incident a Special Forces team was going into an area, and at the last minute we told them their landing zone wasn't the best. We helped change the mission at the last second. Then we helped them find a better place to land'.

STRONG SUPPORT

The bombers, fighters and ground troops typically grab the headlines, but the support assets in an operation as large as 'Iraqi Freedom' are equally important.

The in-flight refuelling tankers proved invaluable for the campaign, with attack and ISR assets relying heavily on the airborne fuel stations after long transits from bases around the region. Tanker crews such as KC-135 pilot Capt Richard Peterson from the 321st Air Expeditionary Wing provided vital support around the clock. He commented 'Life has been a non-stop cycle of fly, crew rest, and time to go again'. Missions routinely stretched from seven to nine hours

Above: **The USAF's KC-10A Extender tankers operated from a number of locations in support of OIF, including Bourgas in Bulgaria.** *USAF*

Below: **Soaking up the warm Mediterranean sun, a line up of USAF KC-135R Stratotankers assigned to the 401st AEW at RAF Akrotiri, Cyprus, sit ready for their next OIF mission.** *USAF*

supporting bombers, fighters and surveillance aircraft hungry for fuel. A total of 149 USAF KC-135s and 33 KC-10s flew 6,193 sorties during the ground war, with an impressive 86.4% mission-capable rate.

Col Cathy Clothier, 401st Air Expeditionary Operations Group commander at RAF Akrotiri, said 'I briefed all our aircrew about the upcoming operations and told them what we were about to do in the next few days would change history. Not a single bomb gets dropped, not a single air-to-air engagement happens, or missile is fired unless tankers make it happen. I'm proud of our people here'.

With as many as 32 KC-135Rs operating from Akrotiri, as well as a number of other assets, the base had been upgraded with new parking ramps to accommodate the large influx of aircraft. Capt Chadd Kobielush deployed from RAF Mildenhall, UK, was also based at the station 'It's rewarding helping the people of Iraq as a pilot refuelling coalition aircraft. It motivates you more when you feel like you're helping out the folks back

Above: **An HH-60G deployed from the 347th Rescue Wing at Moody AFB, GA, takes on fuel from a HC-130P while a second example waits for its turn on the drogue.** *USAF*

Right: **A pair of huge C-5 Galaxy transport aircraft sit on the ramp at Balad in Iraq after the base was captured by Coalition forces. Captured bases were quickly pressed into action to efficiently support the frontline forces.** *USAF*

home. As long as we can neutralise Saddam Hussein that's a good blow to the enemies of America'.

In addition to the KC-135s, KC-10A Extenders were also kept very busy during Operation 'Iraqi Freedom'. The US tanker assets maintain an extremely busy deployed operating schedule, which places a huge strain on aircraft and personnel. Operating from Al Udeid, Qatar; Bourgas, Bulgaria; and Al Dhafra, UAE, the KC-10s supported all Coalition assets during OIF. Even with the RAF tanker support, these assets became in high demand throughout the campaign, with the US Navy's Sixth Fleet being hit hard by a lack of tanker support when the heavy bombers took priority on their longer-range missions.

Heavy haulers

Alongside the tankers, none of 'Iraqi Freedom' would have been possible without the transport fleets that hauled the personnel and equipment to the Persian Gulf and re-supplied the frontline throughout.

The colossal Lockheed Martin C-5 Galaxy is able to carry 36 standard pallets, and 265,000lbs of cargo – roughly double that of the newer C-17. While the C-17 stole the spotlight in Afghanistan and Iraq by bringing troops and equipment directly to the frontlines, the C-5 fleet brought in nearly half (48%) of all cargo required for the campaign. Gen John W. Handy, commander of Air Mobility Command, recalled; 'In this conflict there were many times when frankly the only way to unclog Charleston AFB, Dover AFB or Ramstein AB, Germany, was to get the C-5s in there in sufficient numbers and literally clean out these aerial ports. It has an astounding capability that we certainly need to keep at our fingertips for as far as I can see into the future'.

The versatile USAF Boeing C-17s played a huge part in the US strategic transport effort needed to maintain the hectic

CSAR SPECIALISTS

The highly specialised role of Combat Search and Rescue (CSAR) involves the recovery of personnel – regularly from behind enemy lines – and is one of the most challenging missions facing the US military today. It is a low profile, yet politically important mission that is carried out by dedicated rescue or Special Operations Forces (SOF). The USAF is the world leader in this field.

CSAR often involves a sizable Search And Rescue Task Force (SARTF). This is typically composed of fixed- and rotary-wing aircraft, fighters, tankers and airborne command posts and the structure of each SARTF is dictated by the complexity of the task.

In preparation for OIF, Iraq was divided into CSAR sectors and specific assets were assigned to each. HH-60G Pave Hawks were at Forward Operating Locations (FOL) as close as possible to the action. A force of just 10 HC/MC-130Ps and 16 HH-60Gs from a mix of active component, Air National Guard and Air Force Reserve Command were supplemented by 31 MH-53J/Ms and additional MC-130E/Ps assigned to SOF units.

OIF involved over 17,000 strike missions with 20 Coalition aircraft lost and less than 250 CSAR sorties launched as a result of this low attrition rate. The Joint Search and Rescue Center (JSRC) executed just 55 CSAR missions, which saved 73 personnel and assisted with the rescues of 20 others. Perhaps one of the most dramatic rescues occurred on 8 April 2003 when an A-10A pilot was forced to eject from his stricken jet not far from Baghdad International Airport. A CSAR force was quickly dispatched to successfully recover the pilot.

'ops tempo'. The troop insertion into northern Iraq on 27 March by 15 C-17s was dubbed 'the largest airborne assault since D-Day'. This also marked the first-ever C-17 combat insertion of paratroopers – another of the many aviation 'firsts' of the conflict. Over the five days that followed, the USAF conducted 62 airlift flights and delivered 2,000 personnel, more than 400 vehicles and 3,000 tons of supplies to captured airfields in northern Iraq to support the push south towards Mosul, Iraq's third city. This included M1 Abrams main battle tanks (MBTs) to support the offensive. Such a move was required following Turkey's decision not to support military action, except for allowing overflights. It transpired that the US Army's 4th Infantry Division had planned to move across the border from Turkey, but instead changed course and headed through the Suez Canal to offload its equipment in Kuwait. The forces brought in by C-17s in the north were able to make use of the airfields at Bashur, Arbil, Mosul and Sulaymaniyah – all of which had been captured by Special Forces. This opened up a vital set of bridgeheads to the north of the country, thus allowing the ground force to continue its spear southwards.

Left: Combat Search and Rescue (CSAR) assets were on hand around the clock to rescue downed aircrew and bring them back to safety. The Sikorsky MH-53 Pave Low played a lead role in such operations from the first night of the war. *USAF*

Below: On the flightline at Baghdad International Airport, a Sikorsky HH-60G deployed from the 106th Rescue Wing at Francis S. Gabreski IAP, NY, shares the ramp with a pair of AFSOC MH-53s. *USAF*

United States Navy

The US Navy and US Marine Corps brought a huge force to bear against Iraq. The flexibility of these two branches of the US armed forces allows commanders to react to situations around the world and move a massive fighting force onto the doorstep of the theatre. This conflict proved to be no exception.

The USS *Harry S. Truman* (CVN-75) and USS *Theodore Roosevelt* (CVN-71) operated in the Mediterranean and the USS *Constellation* (CV-64), USS *Kitty Hawk* (CV-63), USS *Abraham Lincoln* (CVN-72) were all deployed to the NAG (Northern Arabian Gulf), with the USS *Nimitz* (CVN-68) joining later to replace the Lincoln.

Above: **Full throttle – the US Navy swung into action right from the outset of OIF. This F-14A Tomcat of VF-154 'Black Knights' is seen in full afterburner seconds prior to launching from the deck of the USS *Kitty Hawk* (CV-63). It was the unit's last cruise with the F-14A Tomcat.** *US Navy*

Left: **Directing an F/A-18C onto the catapult, another wave of missions prepares to depart for Iraq.** *US Navy*

Bottom left: **The mighty USS *Harry S. Truman* (CVN-75), with Carrier Air Wing Three (CVW-3) embarked, operated from the Mediterranean for OIF.** *US Navy*

Each carrier battle group and associated carrier air wing (CVW) has around 11,000 crew embarked. As well as the CVW, the battle group has vessels equipped with Tomahawk cruise missiles.

By mid-April more than 6,500 OIF sorties had been flown from the US Navy carriers, with 64% being strike and close air support (CAS) missions. This was achieved with one fewer carrier and air wing (USS *Nimitz* and CVW-11 arrived right at the end of the war) than in Operation 'Desert Storm' in 1991. Adhering strictly to the modern US Navy maxim of 'quality, not quantity' the effectiveness of the aircraft sent into combat in 2003 more than made up for any shortfall in numbers compared with 'Gulf War I'. The employment of smart weapons such as Joint Direct Attack Munitions (JDAMs),

Above: **The Deputy Carrier Air Wing Commander (DCAG) for CVW-3, Capt Pat 'Irish' Rainey, briefs with a member of the US Navy SEAL Team 8 as well as squadron aircrew aboard the USS *Harry S. Truman* (CVN-75) as the war unfolds.** *US Navy*

Right: **An F-14A pilot from VF-154 prepares for another mission (note LGB 'kill' markings). The squadron sent a shore detachment of four jets to Al Udeid in Qatar during OIF.** *US Navy*

VF-2's new claws

Having deployed on its final 'WestPac' with the F-14D in November 2002, and arrived in the Northern Arabian Gulf (NAG) just prior to Christmas Day, VF-2 'Bounty Hunters' had been frustrated in its attempts to participate in the increased Operation 'Southern Watch' strikes due to its F-14D's JDAM incompatibility. VF-2 CO, CDR Doug Denneny, remembers;

'When VF-2 set sail on 2 November 2002, we were well prepared for potential combat operations. Our 10 F-14Ds were in excellent condition. Our morale was high, and we were pretty confident that our timing was going to be good for what we considered was a foregone conclusion that we would invade Iraq. The biggest disappointment prior to deployment was that our aircraft were not yet configured with a new computer software upgrade referred to as D04, which would allow the delivery of the 2,000lb GBU-31 JDAM. The JDAM uses GPS satellites to hit targets with pinpoint accuracy, not relying on a targeting pod like the LANTIRN. It is a launch and leave weapon, and can be delivered day or night through clouds, unlike the Laser-Guided Bombs that require the LANTIRN to be able to see the

Joint Stand-Off Weapon (JSOW) and new-generation Laser-Guided Bombs (LGBs), allied with better tactics and more versatile aircraft, allowed the US Navy to make a more meaningful and visible contribution this time around.

Driven by the USAF's outstanding use of smart bombs, the US Navy invested significant funds in the 1990s on technologies that ensured 'one weapon, one target destroyed'.

CAT FIGHT

There is no better example of how US naval aviation has evolved for the good than in the employment of the Grumman F-14 Tomcat. Used almost exclusively as an interceptor in 1991, the jet was kept away from the real action because of its inability to conduct Non-Co-operative Target Recognition (NCTR), which saw crews utilising classified radar techniques to identify enemy aircraft by type. With all the 'choice' CAP slots in Iraq given to the USAF's F-15Cs, the Tomcat units were left to fly often tedious defensive CAPs for the fleet and for US Navy strike packages.

By 2003, the Tomcat had been transformed into a true multi-role combat platform that boasted more mission taskings than any other aircraft currently operating from the flightdeck of a US carrier. Capable of precision bombing, buddy laser target designation through use of the LANTIRN pod, Forward Air Controlling (Airborne) (FAC-A), Strike Co-ordinating Armed Reconnaissance (SCAR), photo and digital reconnaissance and, of course, fighter interception, the 56 F-14s that participated in OIF made a far greater contribution than the 100-plus in 'Desert Storm'.

One of the primary weapons employed by the Tomcat in OIF was the GBU-31 2,000lb JDAM. Initially cleared for use by the F-14B only, the JDAM was hastily made compatible with the F-14D through the installation of the D04 weapons computer upgrade in the weeks leading up to OIF. The VF-2 'Bounty Hunters', embarked with CVW-2 on the USS *Constellation* (CV-64), was the first D-model unit to get the upgrade.

ground. During the summer of 2002, while we were in work-ups, NAVAIR found some more problems with the tape, causing a delay. The chain of command and I were not interested in taking an immature tape on cruise, so we left without what we considered an incredibly important warfighting tool'.

It was not until 31 January 2003 that VF-2 was officially notified that its jets would receive the D04 upgrade, which pushed squadron morale 'through the roof' according to CDR Denneny. Four weeks later, on 28 February, the unit dropped its first ever GBU-31 JDAM bombs on a target in southern Iraq — marking the first time an F-14D had used the weapon in combat.

Elsewhere, the F-14Ds of VF-31 'Tomcatters' aboard the USS *Abraham Lincoln* (CVN-72) were reconfigured with D04 straight after VF-2. Assigned to CVW-14, and also operating in the NAG, VF-31 had been on deployment since 20 July 2002. Relieved of the OSW mission by the Constellation Battle Group in December, CVN-71 had got as far east as Perth, Western

Above: **Plugged into the tanker, a VF-2 F-14D replenishes its fuel tanks. The aircraft carries a mixed load of AIM-9M Sidewinders, a LANTIRN pod and an AIM-54C Phoenix.** *US Navy*

Left: **An F-14D of VF-2 'Bounty Hunters' returns to the USS *Constellation* (CV-64) following a successful mission over Iraq.** *US Navy*

Australia, when it was turned around and sent back to the Gulf as part of the build up for OIF.

The final Tomcat unit to receive the D04 mission tape upgrade was VF-213 'Black Lions', operating from the USS *Theodore Roosevelt* (CVN-71) in the Mediterranean Sea. It too got to train with JDAM in the weeks immediately prior to OIF. Of the two remaining Tomcat squadrons committed to the conflict, VF-32, again in the Mediterranean aboard USS *Harry S. Truman* (CVN-75), had had its F-14Bs modified to become JDAM-compatible prior to deployment, but the baseline F-14A models assigned to VF-154, flying from the USS *Kitty Hawk* (CV-63) in the NAG, remained restricted to LGBs.

'Shock and Awe'

The 'Bounty Hunters' were at the forefront of OIF from the word go, participating in the 'Shock and Awe' strikes on Baghdad throughout the opening nights of the war. Indeed, CVW-2 provided the lead Coalition strike force to hit targets in the Iraqi capital, its Tomcats dropping JDAMs as well as performing the defensive counter air and reconnaissance missions for the remaining CVW-2 assets.

Amongst the targets assigned to the unit on the opening night of the war was the Salman Pak AM Transmitter Radio Relay Facility at Al Hurriyah, southwest of Baghdad. It was hit by two F-14Ds and two F/A-18Cs, as well as by HARM-equipped F-16CJs and F/A-18Cs and numerous other support aircraft outside the MEZ (Missile Exclusion Zone) that were

unleashing JSOWs and other guided weapons. Crews reported seeing continuous AAA following an impressive, non-stop TLAM (Tomahawk Land Attack Missile) and CALCM (Conventional Air-Launched Cruise Missile) attack. After the Tomahawks had stopped, the CVW-2 jets, led by VF-2 CO CDR Denneny, became the first non-stealth strike package to venture into Baghdad's 'Super MEZ', where they were engaged by up to a dozen unguided SAMs and non-stop AAA. Nonetheless, the target was destroyed and the jets all got back safely.

Operating from Fifth Fleet's designated OIF night carrier, VF-2 proceeded to fly the bulk of its missions masked by the cover of

Below: **An amazing shot through the LANTIRN targeting pod of a GBU-24 laser-guided bomb as it is released from an F-14B of VF-32 over Iraq.** *US Navy*

darkness. It initially used JDAMs to hit fixed targets such as command and control nodes, SAM and radar sites, airfields and Republican Guard barracks, as well as presidential palaces and Ba'ath Party buildings. The Tomcat squadron then switched to CAS strikes as the ground push towards Baghdad gained momentum. The Tomcat's ability to perform the demanding FAC-A and SCAR roles was also greatly appreciated as Coalition forces engaged the Republican Guard around cities such as Karbala and An Nasiriyah. CDR Denneny recalls; 'By the end of March FAC-A events were going on in earnest. I soon became a little concerned that some of the guys were getting down too low – very dangerous – the big Tomcat is a heck of a target. I told them only to go low if it was the only thing left to do, and that it would directly save the lives of our troops on the ground. Early April saw us flying lots of support missions for troops heading for Karbala, where we took out a Tu-124 'Cookpot' on a runway. We were also flying lots of SCAR missions up there, providing the FAC-A for B-52s and other Coalition assets'.

Aside from tactical strike missions, VF-2 completed its share of defensive counter air sorties and reconnaissance flights for CVW-2 as well. Reverting to precision strikers when needed, one of the unit's more interesting targets in the latter stages of the war was Saddam Hussein's presidential yacht, which was bombed in Basra harbour (see battle damage chapter).

During the 28 days of OIF, VF-2 successfully completed 195 combat sorties totalling 887.5 hours. Its 10 aircraft dropped 221 LGBs (217 GBU-12s and 4 GBU-16s) and 61 GBU-31 JDAMs. Some 1,704 20mm cannon rounds were also fired in strafing

passes and no fewer than 125 targets were photographed using the TARPS reconnaissance system.

The other Tomcat squadrons in the NAG also flew a broad mix of missions ranging from precision strikes to CAS and FAC-A. The 'Tomcatters' of VF-31 flew from USS *Abraham Lincoln* (CVN-72), which was the designated day carrier. The unit operated closely with fellow CVW-14 squadron VFA-115, which was conducting its very first cruise with the Boeing F/A-18E Super Hornet. With the latter jet boasting Tomcat-like endurance, VF-31 often flew mixed strike missions with VFA-115, as well as the four forward-deployed Super Hornets from CVW-11's VFA-14 'Tophatters' and VFA-41 'Black Aces'. Answering a Central Command request for additional strike and tanker assets, the Nimitz Battle Group had despatched four jets to CVN-72 on 30-31 March. These F/A-18E/F Super Hornets were paired with VF-31's Tomcats because the F-14 crews were flying predominantly FAC-A and SCAR missions by early April. A single VFA-41 jet would typically operate as the wingman for a solitary Tomcat, the crews being 'shown the ropes' in-theatre by the combat-seasoned 'Tomcatters'. The pairing up of the F-14D and the F/A-18F was done primarily because the VFA-41 aircraft were taking missions that would have been assigned to VF-31 in the daily ATO (Air Tasking Order). CVW-14 considered this the most expeditious way to get the additional F/A-18Fs into action.

By the time CVN-72 and CVW-14 were relieved in-theatre by CVN-68 and CVW-11 on 14 April, VF-31 had flown an astounding 585 combat sorties and 1,744 combat hours during its marathon 10-month OEF/OSW/OIF deployment. The unit had delivered 56 JDAMs, 165 GBU-12s, five GBU-16s, 13 Mk 82 'dumb' bombs and 1,355 rounds of 20mm cannon fire.

Below: **A VF-31 'Tomcatters' F-14D emblazoned with OIF mission marks taxies to the catapult aboard USS *Abraham Lincoln* (CVN-72).** *US Navy*

Above: **The 'Black Knights' of VF-154 were tasked by CENTCOM to detach four F-14As and four crews to provide dedicated FAC-A and SCAR support for USAF, RAF and RAAF fast jets flying out of Al Udeid, Qatar. OIF became the first conflict in recent history to see the US Navy simultaneously fight from land and sea.** *No 12(B) Squadron RAF*

Left: **The unmistakable sight of an F-14A in full burner. This example is from VF-154 'Black Knights' aboard the USS *Kitty Hawk* (CV-63).** *US Navy*

procedures in OSW, VF-154 completed a number of successful missions into Iraq in the lead-up to war.

It was whilst conducting these combat sorties alongside USAF assets in the Gulf that the unit was asked by Central Command to detach four aircraft and four crews to provide dedicated FAC-A and SCAR support for USAF, RAF and RAAF fast jets flying out of Al Udeid, Qatar. Aside from performing these missions, the VF-154 Tomcat crews, led by squadron CO CDR James H. Flatley, were also given the responsibility of instructing their F-15E brethren from the 336th FS/4th FW on how to conduct effective FAC-A and SCAR.

According to VF-154's post-cruise summary of its contribution to OIF, 'Never in recent history had a carrier-based strike-fighter squadron been tasked to fight a war from ashore and at sea at the same time. The 'Black Knights' specialist FAC-A crews at Al Udeid amassed more than 300 combat hours and delivered more than 50,000lb of ordnance in 21 days of flying with their four crews and four jets'.

The unit did not escape from its shore-based foray unscathed. On the night of 1 April, pilot Lt Chad Vincelette and RIO LCDR Scotty McDonald were forced to eject over southern Iraq when their jet (F-14A BuNo 158620) suffered a single (port) engine and fuel transfer system failure. The latter caused the remaining 'good' engine to run dry, so the crew, two hours into their mission (and having already dropped some of their LGBs) were forced to 'bang out' over hostile territory and were thankfully quickly retrieved by a CSAR team from Kuwait.

The shore detachment returned to CV-63 in the second week of April, and by the end of the aerial campaign on 14 April, VF-154 had dropped 358 LGBs during the course of 286 combat sorties.

Above: **Red-shirted ordnancemen assemble racks of 2,000lb GBU-31 Joint Direct Attack Munitions (JDAMs) for loading on F-14B Tomcats of VF-32 'Swordsmen' aboard USS *Harry S. Truman* (CVN-75).** *US Navy*

'Black Knights'

Unable to employ JDAMs with its F-14As, the war fought by VF-154 'Black Knights' was undoubtedly the most unusual of any of the Tomcat units committed to OIF. Deployed on its final cruise with the F-14 as part of CVW-5, the 'Black Knights' ventured into the NAG with the Kitty Hawk in mid-February 2003 – the first time that CVW-5 had operated in the region since 1999. Despite its relative unfamiliarity with current operating

Tomcats 'in the Med'

The OIF war waged by the two Mediterranean-based carriers contrasted markedly with that fought by the vessels sailing in the NAG, as CVW-3's Public Affairs Officer Lt Jason Rojas explained in the air wing's cruise summary; 'The war over northern Iraq was quite different from the one in the south. With Turkey denying the US Army's 4th Infantry Division use of its territory as a jumping-off point, northern-front activities centred around Special Operations Forces (SOF) activity, with some teams as small as three individuals. The teams relied heavily on CAS from CVW-3 and CVW-8, the latter embarked in the USS *Theodore Roosevelt* (CVN-71), which was also positioned in the eastern Mediterranean. Aircraft from both air wings flew CAS missions in support of SOF units, often putting ordnance dangerously close to friendly forces. The support these aircraft provided undoubtedly saved the lives of Coalition forces on the ground, and eventually led to the capitulation of nearly 100,000 Iraqi soldiers'.

Prior to immersing itself in CAS missions with SOF, both VF-32 'Swordsmen' and VF-213 'Black Lions' completed a number of conventional strikes with JDAMs and LGBs against fixed targets in Iraq. These sorties, flown at the start of the conflict, were some of the longest of the war, covering distances of up to 800 miles each way. As the Tomcat had proven in Operation 'Enduring Freedom' in 2001-02, it was more than capable of handling such

sorties, and the F-14 crews often flew the mission lead for these more conventional strikes. Indeed, the first CVW-3 mission of the war was led by 'Desert Storm 'veteran, and VF-32 CO, CDR Marcus Hitchcock. He explained the complex routing problems that the carrier air wings in the eastern Mediterranean had to grapple with for the first 72 hours of the war.

'In the lead up to our first mission, the political situation in our area was a little topsy-turvy to say the least. We didn't know whether we would be heading in via Turkey or not. This meant that we had to plan a series of different routes into Iraq – northerly, central and southerly. The diplomats finally settled on us going south from the Mediterranean, across both the Saudi Arabian peninsula and the Gulf of Aquaba, back up into Saudi Arabia once again, around Jordan and then finally into Iraq. Approval for this route was given just 24hrs before the start of OIF, and a lot of the supporting tanker assets were not given the word that they needed to be in a certain location in order to facilitate our first strikes. Nineteen aircraft – six of which were supporting E-2s and S-3s – launched on the first mission, and 13 proceeded south to Iraq. Our tanking with USAF assets en-route was interesting to say the least, as the KC-135s showed up at the designated rendezvous point so late that we were reaching the decision point on whether to divert jets because they were running out of gas! Two of the Hornets were 'timed out' and could not press into Iraq. Pre-OIF, we had trained with

Above: **Low down over the Mediterranean, a VF-32 'Swordsmen' F-14B heads back to the USS *Harry S. Truman* (CVN-75) after an OIF daylight strike mission.** *US Navy*

Left: **A fine study of the VF-32 'Swordmen' CAG jet as it conducts a mission during OIF.** *US Navy*

our Tomcats loaded up with three JDAMs. No other unit had sortied with more than two weapons up to that point, as the jet was very heavy on the controls at cruising altitude when fuelled for combat, carrying defensive missiles and three 2,000lb bombs. We trained hard in this configuration once in the Med, and this training paid off in OIF.

'Hitting our airfield target on that first night, my crews did spectacular work with their JDAMs. We knew about the weapon's capability in theory, but it was not until we had each delivered our three bombs smack onto our targets, spread across the airfield, within a matter of seconds that it became readily apparent that this was a new kind of weapon the likes of which we had never seen before'.

Further strikes on conventional targets followed and the mission times reduced slightly once Turkey permitted overflights. CVW-3 operated from the designated day carrier, whilst CVW-8 handled much of the night work. The 'Black Lions' of VF-213 soon dubbed its nocturnal missions 'Vampire' sorties, with jets regularly launching from the pitch-black deck of CVN-71 into poor weather conditions. The constant night operations eventually inspired the aircrew to coin the phrase 'living after midnight, bombing 'til dawn'!

One of the more unusual missions flown by VF-213 saw the unit providing CAP for the airborne landings made by a thousand paratroopers of the US Army's 173rd Airborne Brigade. Conducting the largest parachute drop since WW2, the soldiers jumped from a fleet of C-17s into Kurdish-controlled northern Iraq. The Globemasters were escorted by three waves of strike aircraft from CVN-71, with the US Navy jets also bombing Iraqi command and control bunkers and troop and artillery positions close to nearby Bashur airfield.

As the war progressed, CAS for Special Forces squads became the staple mission for both VF-32 and VF-213, and their success in this role was related by CVW-8's CAG, Capt David Newland; 'Dropping precision-guided ordnance for a SOF team was a mission that gave immediate gratification. They were told where to drop the munitions, and they got direct feedback from the troops after they had dropped'.

By the time VF-213 ceased combat operations in OIF on 15 April, its crews had flown 198 combat sorties and 907.6 combat flight hours, with a 100% sortie completion rate. A total of 196 precision-guided bombs weighing 250,000lb had been expended, with 102 of these being LGBs and the remaining being 94 JDAMs. VF-32 completed an impressive 268 sorties and 1135.2 hours in combat, dropping 247 LGBs and 118 JDAMs (402,600lb). Its crews also expended 1,128 rounds of 20mm high explosive incendiary in strafing passes.

Below: **A trio of F-14Ds sits on deck ready for action as other air wing aircraft streak past upon their recovery to the ship.** *US Navy*

Left: **Eagles' break – a VFA-115 'Eagles' Boeing F/A-18E Super Hornet armed with a pair of GBU-31 JDAMs breaks for action. The US Navy greatly benefited from the new capabilities offered by the Super Hornet. The type's increased ordnance 'bring-back' capability, its two extra wing stations and the larger internal fuel capacity paid dividends.** *US Navy*

Below: **The VFA-115 'Eagles' 'CAG-Bird' F/A-18E prepares to launch from the USS *Abraham Lincoln* (CVN-72) armed with 'slick' Mk82 bombs and an LGB.** *US Navy*

HORNET'S STING

Some 250 Boeing F/A-18 Hornets were committed to 'Iraqi Freedom', with almost 200 of these being US Navy and attached US Marine Corps carrier-based examples. This strike fighter was truly the 'universal soldier' of the air war. Having borne the brunt of the US Navy's OSW campaign, and several other significant conflicts since 'Desert Storm', the F/A-18s in action for OIF were vastly superior in their ability to wage precision warfare than their more austere forebears of 1991.

The combat debut of the F/A-18E/F Super Hornet in the lead up to OIF graphically demonstrated just how much the F/A-18 had matured in 12 years. VFA-115 'Eagles', embarked in the USS *Abraham Lincoln* (CVN-72), was given the task of blooding naval aviation's latest weapon, and it duly flew more than 200 Operation 'Enduring Freedom' and 'Southern Watch' combat missions with its new F/A-18Es prior to 'Iraqi Freedom'. According to the squadron's cruise report; 'The unit carried an impressive array of air-to-air and air-to-ground weapons and proved the most reliable strike platform in either theatre. In short, VFA-115 did what it set out to accomplish; integrate the Super Hornet into the fleet, and support CVW-14's mission by utilising the new aircraft's capabilities to the fullest possible extent'.

The Super Hornet's ability to carry more fuel and additional ordnance made it ideally suited for the previous operations over Afghanistan, although it did not get to employ ordnance during that time. That all changed once CVN-72 moved into the NAG, and on 6 November 2002 Lt John Turner made history in F/A-18E BuNo 165783 when he and his wingman dropped four JDAMs on Iraqi SAM launchers at Al Kut and a command and control bunker at Tallil. Further attacks followed 24hrs later, and then again on 10 November. Such strikes meant that by the time OIF commenced a few months later in March, VFA-115 was more than prepared for combat. As the war kicked off, the 'Eagles' were quick to showcase the

capability of the Super Hornet. The type's increased ordnance bring-back capability; two extra wing stations and a larger internal fuel capacity were big improvements.

The capability for a single aircraft to deliver 8,000lb of ordnance to four targets allowed a section of Super Hornets to perform what in the past would have required two divisions (eight jets). In addition, the extra fuel on board allowed single-cycle CAS missions deep into Iraq while maintaining an impressive 4,000lb loadout of recoverable ordnance.

The squadron also performed the less glamorous (but no less important) role of aerial tanking. This mission was thrust upon VFA-115 when it became clear that the prosecution of the air war would be hampered by a lack of airborne tankers. Providing organic air wing tanking for CVW-14, the 'Eagles' began flying 18-20 refuelling sorties a day on top of its continuing cycle of strike missions. Since one Super Hornet tanker could provide fuel to two strike aircraft, the squadron's efforts, in conjunction with the S-3Bs of VS-35, facilitated about 40 sorties per day from CVN-72. By war's end VFA-115 had passed 2.3m lb of fuel, generating more than 430 extra combat sorties. Flying more than 5,400 hours, and delivering 460,000lb of ordnance, the 'Eagles' integrated the Super Hornet into fleet operations in a remarkable fashion.

Coming forward

A lack of tankers, and the undoubted success of the Super Hornet, led Central Command to ask CVW-11, which was embarked in the USS *Nimitz* (CVN-68), for additional help. The carrier was still some 4,300 miles (two weeks sailing time) away from the NAG at the time, steaming westwards across

Left: **A quartet of VFA-41 F/A-18F Super Hornets (known by crews as 'Rhinos'). As the USS *Nimitz* (CVN-68) steamed towards the NAG, VFA-41 'Black Aces' and VFA-14 'Tophatters' each sent a pair of jets ahead to the USS *Abraham Lincoln* (CVN-72). All four aircraft were soon flying combat missions as part of CVW-14 aboard the Lincoln, with the VFA-14 jets remaining 'plumbed' as tankers and the VFA-41 aircraft undertaking FAC-A and SCAR sorties.** *US Navy*

Bottom: **Sunset Super Hornet – an F/A-18F of VFA-41 'Black Aces' cruises at altitude. Note that the pilot wears the significantly larger Joint Helmet Mounted Cueing System (JHMCS).** *US Navy*

the Indian Ocean. Keen to help, CVW-11 despatched four aircraft – two F/A-18Es from VFA-14 'Tophatters' and two F/A-18Fs from VFA-41 'Black Aces', the latter manned by FAC-A qualified crews. With each aircraft carrying four underwing tanks and a centreline aerial refuelling store, the Super Hornets headed for the USS *Abraham Lincoln* (CVN-72), via an overnight stop in Diego Garcia.

All four aircraft were soon flying combat missions with CVW-14, the VFA-14 jets remaining plumbed as tankers and the VFA-41 F/A-18Fs undertaking FAC-A and SCAR sorties.

One of the more challenging missions carried out by the jets is detailed by VFA-41's LCDR Mark Weisgerber; 'The difficulties of supporting troops in this conflict became apparent when they started taking fire from paramilitary forces using light trucks to pick at their flanks. For us, it was very difficult to distinguish between paramilitary forces and innocent civilians travelling along the roads. The conundrum was that the enemy was using suicide bomber tactics, i.e. trying to crash their explosive-laden vehicles into our Marines. Our solution was to

strafe in front of vehicles that were closing on the Marine convoy with any speed, a sort of warning shot across the bow. If the vehicle continued to close to within one kilometre, then we would destroy it with a laser-guided weapon. Our flight completed three strafing runs on two separate trucks during one sortie, and both pulled over to the side of the road after they saw the bullets impacting in front of them – they don't know how lucky they were!'

The jets returned to the Nimitz on 6 April, and the carrier finally relieved CVN-72 eight days later. In the final throes of the aerial campaign, VFA-41 debuted the SHared Reconaissance Pod (SHARP) and, along with VFA-14, the Joint Helmet Mounted Cueing System (JHMCS) and the production-standard Advanced Tactical Forward-Looking Infra-Red (ATFLIR) system – all crucial systems for the future.

Top: A pair of 'Black Aces' F/A-18Fs conducts in-flight refuelling training over Iraq following CVW-11's arrival in the NAG aboard USS *Nimitz* (CVN-68). *US Navy*

Centre left: Ready to support troops on the ground, a GBU-12-armed 'Black Aces' F/A-18F maintains station over Baghdad International Airport during OIF. *US Navy*

Left: 'War Party' – a VFA-87 'Golden Warriors' F/A-18C plugs in full afterburner as it prepares for a night launch from the USS *Theodore Roosevelt* (CVN-71). Hosting Carrier Air Wing Eight (CVW-8), CVN-71 operated in the eastern Mediterranean during OIF. *US Navy*

Top right: This VFA-41 'Black Aces' F/A-18F Super Hornet is heavily laden in tanker configuration. *US Navy*

Right: Seen trapping aboard the USS *Abraham Lincoln* (CVN-72), a VFA-25 'Fist of the Fleet' F/A-18C returns to the ship with its weapons. If crews couldn't positively identify a target, they did not drop their bombs. *US Navy*

Right: Deployed as part of CVW-8, VFA-201 'Hunters' was the first US Navy Reserve unit to be mobilised since the end of the Korean War. The Fort Worth JRB-based F/A-18A+ Hornet squadron was staffed by highly experienced pilots (whose average age was 35 with 350 carrier landings and 2,700 flying hours in their log books). The unit led 25% of all OIF sorties conducted from the USS *Theodore Roosevelt* (CVN-71). *Jamie Hunter/aviacom*

Reserves at war

The bulk of the F/A-18s in theatre were 'legacy' C-models, although Reserve-manned VFA-201 and the US Marine Corps' VMFA-115, operating in the Mediterranean with CVW-8 and CVW-3 respectively, flew the upgraded F/A-18A+. The latter boasts an APG-73 radar, full LGB and JDAMs weapons capability and improved ECM and RWR systems.

Becoming the first US Navy Reserve unit to be mobilised since the end of the Korean War, Fort Worth JRB-based VFA-201 'Hunters' made good use of its newly-acquired F/A-18A+ Hornets in the nocturnal war fought by CVW-8. Staffed by highly experienced pilots whose average age was 35 with 350 carrier landings and 2,700 flying hours in their logbooks, the unit proceeded to lead 25% of all OIF sorties conducted from CVN-71.

One of the most memorable missions for the 'Hunters' involved CDR Sean Clark and CDR Alan Beal who, on the night of 31 March, supported a British Special Forces squad that was operating in western Iraq. The unit's position had reportedly been compromised and the team had retreated into central Iraq, fending off a large enemy force hunting them down.

A pair of VFA-201 Hornets launched from the Roosevelt as 'Cujo flight', refuelled from a KC-135R and were told by an E-3 AWACS to proceed over 200 miles south into western Iraq to relieve a pair of USAF F-16s which had been searching for the unit. The 'Hunters' pilots were passed co-ordinates for a general area. CDR Clark takes up the story; 'After

Above: A VFA-201 'Hunters' Hornet armed with LGBs and JDAMs heads for Iraq as the sun sinks. This Naval Reserve squadron flew night missions as part of CVW-8. *US Navy*

Below: US Navy F/A-18Cs regularly fly with asymmetric loads. This example carries an AGM-154 Joint Stand-Off Weapon (JSOW) on the port side and a 330USGal fuel tank on the starboard. *USN via USAF*

approximately 30mins of searching, 'Cujo flight' picked up a faint IR (infra-red) strobe and started a descent to lower altitude to verify the position. Upon verification, and subsequently marking the position of the strobe, I told the AWACS that the unit had been found. With fuel running critically low, we were forced to return (to the tanker) to refuel. We then headed back overhead as USAF rescue forces were launched. While overhead, we detected Iraqi vehicles proceeding near the search area. The Iraqis were also looking for the unit, and they began searching in close proximity to them with flashlights. Sensing that the Iraqi Army was getting too close, we began a descent to 'buzz' the enemy and scare them off. After two low altitude, high-speed passes the Iraqis retreated, got back in their vehicles and drove out of the search area. After approximately 45mins, USAF rescue units, including A-10s, appeared on station. CDR Beal and I remained overhead the rescue effort to provide CAS should the need arise to suppress any Iraqi advance. Reaching critical fuel levels, we then passed the suppression role over to the A-10s, who had now visually acquired the British unit. After seven hours of flight time, and recovery to the carrier, we learned that the unit was safe'.

Hornets downtown

Back in the NAG, the nine carrier-based Hornet units took the fight from the Al-Faw peninsula all the way up to Baghdad and beyond. Hornets from all three air wings flew countless CAS sorties in support of mechanised elements of the US Army's 3rd Infantry Division on 3 and 4 April as they endeavoured to seize Saddam International Airport, situated just 12 miles south-west of Baghdad. One of the pilots involved in these missions was LCDR Zeno Rausa, a Hornet pilot on the staff of CVW-2. He remembers; 'My most satisfying mission took place at Saddam International Airport the night our troops were taking it over. We were directed to strike an artillery piece that was shooting at friendlies on the ground. It was difficult finding the target, and took several passes at lower altitude to identify it. AAA was active both to the west and to the east of our position. At one AAA site several miles east, a coalition aircraft working on a different frequency was down low, weaving amidst the tracers from a battery of three AAA sites, all firing in unison. The same was happening to another aircraft, which was also down low near Al Taqqadum, although it was dodging even larger AAA shells. I found it uncomfortable trying to eyeball the AAA whilst having to simultaneously perform lots of heads-down time staring at the FLIR in order to pinpoint the target. I had a 'nugget' pilot with me, and was glad we didn't

Above left: A 'Yellow Shirt' deck marshaller guides a VFA-37 'Bulls' F/A-18C onto the 'Cat' ready to launch from the USS *Harry S. Truman* (CVN-75). *US Navy*

Above: Bombed up and ready for action – a line-up of fully-armed CVW-5 F/A-18Cs aboard the USS *Kitty Hawk* (CV-63). *US Navy*

Bottom: A naval aviator of VFA-113 'Stingers' checks AIM-120 AMRAAMs as he performs external checks on his F/A-18C Hornet. *US Navy*

63

have to go too low. Scouts on the ground passed target co-ordinates to a ground FAC who then relayed them to us. I advised the scouts to stay well clear of the artillery piece, which had stopped firing presumably because the Iraqis had heard us overhead. The gun was still hot though, and easily identifiable on the FLIR once we had correlated its position.

'I set up for a level release and guided a GBU-12 500lb LGB, which hit the target and sent shards of steel flying into the dust. But my bomb was a dud, so I talked my wingman in to finish the job. His scored a direct hit with good detonation and devastating effects. LGBs are extremely accurate. Knowing that we had helped the troops below was very rewarding'.

Responsible for delivering the bulk of the US Navy's LGBs and JDAMs during the 31 days of fully blown conflict in March and April 2003, the Hornet's OIF mission continues into 2004. On 9 January, for example, two F/A-18Cs from CVW-1's VFA-86, embarked on the USS *Enterprise* (CVN-65), attacked a mortar position manned by Iraqi militants near Balad, north of Baghdad. Both jets dropped a single GBU-32 1,000lb JDAM in the first attack performed by CVW-1 since 28 November 2003. Much larger strikes were undertaken at the end of April 2004, mainly by the CVW-7 assets aboard the USS *George Washington* (CVN-73), when US Marine ground troops needed air support as trouble flared in the unsettled hotspot of Fallujah.

Above: In a holding pattern high above Iraq during a close air support (CAS) mission, a VFA-105 'Gunslingers' CO CDR Tom Lalor takes time out for a quick self-portrait, with his GBU-12-toting wingman in the background. *US Navy*

Right: 'Cat shot' – a Hornet powers off the deck for a strike mission. *US Navy*

Below: The stacked deck of the USS *Abraham Lincoln* (CVN-72), seen as a wave of missions depart in support of OIF. *US Navy*

ON THE PROWL

The Northrop Grumman EA-6B Prowler squadrons involved in OIF provided vital Suppression of Enemy Air Defence (SEAD) missions as well as stand-off jamming. The 35 Prowlers involved in OIF performed such an outstanding job that not a single Coalition aircraft fell to radar-guided SAMs or radar-guided AAA.

Operating alongside the US Marine Corps units VMAQ-1 and VMAQ-2, USAF/US Navy expeditionary squadron VAQ-142 'Gray Wolves' operated from Prince Sultan AB (PSAB) in Saudi Arabia as part of the 363rd Air Expeditionary Wing. In Turkey, VAQ-134 'Garudas' and Reserve-manned VAQ-209 'Star Warriors' were left to kick their heels at Incirlik, prevented from participating in OIF by the Turkish government. The latter unit transferred at least two of its aircraft to the two carriers in the Mediterranean when OIF started.

The PSAB squadrons, with 14 EA-6Bs, were kept busy, typically launching with AGM-88C HARM II-equipped F-16CJs to further enhance radar-killing capabilities. The Fighting Falcon pilots relied on the Prowler ECMOs to feed them target co-ordinates once an active Iraqi radar or SAM site had been detected.

All five embarked squadrons also flew sorties around the clock. In the NAG, the 'seaborne EW mission' was shared between VAQ-131 on the USS *Constellation* (CV-64), VAQ-136 on the USS *Kitty Hawk* (CV-63) and VAQ-139 on the USS *Abraham Lincoln* (CVN-72). Fortunately for these units, some key technical improvements had been worked into their venerable Prowlers prior to deployment, including the installation of green cockpit lighting to facilitate the employment of Night Vision Devices (NVD) as well as USQ-113 communications jamming and Genex decoy jamming

Top: **Joint US Navy/USAF Expeditionery EA-6B Prowler squadron VAQ-142 'Gray Wolves' operated from Prince Sultan AB, Saudi Arabia, during OIF.** *Jamie Hunter/aviacom*

Above: **Some 35 Northrop Grumman EA-6B Prowlers saw action in Operation 'Iraqi Freedom', operating in the vital Suppression of Enemy Air Defence (SEAD) and stand-off jamming roles. The type's potent mission equipment ensured that no Iraqi radar-guided Surface to Air Missiles or Anti-Aircraft Artillery would claim any Coalition aircraft.** *US Navy*

equipment. This allowed the Prowlers to jam even the smallest of systems, including mobile telephones.

The well-publicised F-117 'decapitation mission' (see pages 25-26) saw VAQ-131 'Lancers' launch with less than an hour's notice. Further south, another Prowler from the unit supplied SAM suppression for F/A-18Cs from CVW-2 that bombed targets around Basra. The following day OIF commenced in earnest, as VAQ-131's Lt Ken Velez recalls; 'Shock and Awe! Constellation continued to make history as her battle group initiated the massive air strike campaign during the first official day of OIF. Aided by the use of NVDs, 'Lancer' Prowlers manoeuvred to avoid threats as they supported strikes on Iraq's presidential palaces and key strategic targets in Baghdad'.

The unit did not get to fire its first AGM-88 HARM until 27 March when, late in the afternoon, a SAM site was engaged

Right: **A VAQ-136 'Gauntlets' EA-6B launches in dramatic fashion from the USS *Kitty Hawk* (CV-63). The squadron was embarked as part of CVW-5 and is home based at NAF Atsugi, Japan.** *US Navy*

south of Baghdad during a radar jamming mission. The crew received a short-order tasking from its controlling AWACS to fire a HARM so as to protect other strike aircraft within their assigned combat area.

VAQ-136 'Gauntlets' was also an important player in the aerial campaign in the south, as Lt Tom Clarity explained; 'The 'Gauntlets' logged more than 500hrs during the course of 105 combat missions flown over just 26 days. Proving that an old dog can learn new tricks, VAQ-136 flew more than 1,000hrs on NVDs during the cruise, these having only been added to the jet in January 2003. Crews regularly flew sorties that lasted in excess of six hours, flexing their missions from SEAD to electronic attack, CAS and coverage for SOF teams, often within a single flight.

In the hours leading up to OIF, the 'Gauntlets' flew extended missions to support the insertion of ground forces on the Al-Faw peninsula.

VAQ-139 'Cougars' was also in action from the first night, flying 61 combat missions totalling over 300 hours. The unit also expended 17 HARM rounds.

Below: **Hook down and ready to come aboard, an EA-6B Prowler of VAQ-135 'Black Ravens' prepares to return to USS *Nimitz* (CVN-68) following a mission in support of OIF.** *US Navy*

Little has been reported on the role played by the two Prowler units committed to OIF from CVN-71 and CVN-75, sailing in the eastern Mediterranean. Having said that, CVW-3's VAQ-130 and VAQ-141 of CVW-8 clearly had a very active war as they fired far more AGM-88C HARM missiles than any of the Prowler units operating in the NAG. Quite what these were targeted at remains undisclosed, although the fact that the Iraqi airfields and SAM/radar sites in the north had remained pretty well untouched since 'Desert Storm' (unlike those in the south) may explain why these two units were kept so busy. Operating closely with Special Forces and Kurdish freedom fighters, VAQ-141 'Shadowhawks' expended no fewer than 22 AGM-88Cs, and was instrumental in the successful employment of 42 others by CVW-8's trio of Hornet units. CVW-3's VAQ-130 'Zappers' also got through its supply of HARMs, launching some 36 missiles and helping the Truman's three F/A-18 squadrons fire a further 12 HARMs.

VIKINGS ATTACK!

A Lockheed Martin S-3B Viking of VS-38 'Red Griffins' and two US Navy F/A-18C Hornets from VFA-151 'Vigilantes' from CVW-2, aboard the USS *Constellation* (CV-64), were involved in an historic mission over Iraq on 25 March. One of the Hornets independently identified and destroyed two naval targets before the second Hornet assisted the Viking in an attack on a third.

The F/A-18C acted as the laser designator for the S-3B, which fired a laser-guided AGM-65E Maverick against the target that was operating in the Tigris River near Basra. The F/A-18 provided laser illumination throughout the target engagement.

This event was the first time that the S-3 had received tasking for an overland strike in its 30-year history. In addition, it was also the first time that the type had fired a laser-guided missile in combat. It may also prove to be the last time that the Viking ever fires a missile in anger as it nears retirement from the US Navy, replaced in the tanker role by the Super Hornet.

Below: **The 'Red Griffins' of VS-38 operating from USS *Constellation* (CV-64) were involved in an historic mission over Iraq on 25 March. A squadron S-3B Viking fired a laser-guided AGM-65E Maverick against a target near Basra. This was the first time that an S-3 had received orders to attack a land-based target since the type entered service 30 years ago. It will also probably be its last combat engagement, as the Viking is near the end of its US Navy career.** *US Navy*

Above: 'In short' to trap aboard the USS *Theodore Roosevelt* (CVN-71), an E-2C Hawkeye of VAW-124 'Bear Aces' returns from a mission. The E-2s in OIF not only protected the fleet by flying early warning (AEW) missions but also supported ground troops during very long-endurance missions over Iraq. The E-2's AN/APS-145 radar was used to spot ground targets. Also of note, VAW-117 'Wallbangers' became the first unit to deploy with the upgraded Hawkeye 2000, flying as part of CVW-11 aboard the USS *Nimitz* (CVN-68) during OIF. *Jamie Hunter/aviacom*

Left: The US Navy's latest helicopter, the Sikorsky MH-60S, was in action during OIF with HC-5 'Providers' conducting vertical replenishment (VERTREP) missions. *US Navy*

Below: SPECWAR at work – US Navy special operations warfare (SPECWAR) unit HCS-5 'Firehawks' deployed its HH-60Hs from NAS North Island, CA, in support of OIF. Here, the squadron is seen operating near the prominent Martyr's Memorial in Baghdad. *US Navy*

Right: The P-3 provided vital surveillance capabilities for the Coalition during OIF. As well as US Navy examples in theatre, the Royal Australian AF also deployed with the type. Here, a US Navy crew get low-down over the Ocean to check out a possible maritime threat. *US Navy*

Centre right: US Navy test squadron VX-30 'Bloodhounds' from NBVC Point Mugu, CA, deployed for a very special role in OIF. 'Bloodhounds' skipper CDR Wade 'Torch' Knudson trained up as a C-130 captain and deployed with a squadron DC-130 to Ali al Salem AB, Kuwait, ready for the start of OIF. The DC-130 was employed launching BQM-34 Firebee target drones near Baghdad to drop radar-jamming chaff and to circle the city as decoys to draw anti-aircraft fire away from coalition strike aircraft. One of these achieved some notoriety as its parachute was seen by local Iraqi militia descending into a reed bed in the Tigris River in downtown Baghdad. Graphic TV pictures showed the Iraqis firing into the reeds as they believed the parachute to be from a downed airmen, but most are agreed this was probably a parachute from a Firebee drone. *Jamie Hunter/aviacom*

Below: US Navy P-3C Orion squadrons VP-1 'Screaming Eagles', VP-40 'Fighting Marlins', VP-46 'Gray Knights' and VP-47 'Golden Swordsmen' deployed for OIF. Regularly flying missions armed with AGM-65 Mavericks, the P-3C AIP (Aircraft Improvement Program) versions were able to employ their long-range optical surveillance systems to provide targeting for Coalition forces, including USAF AC-130 gunships. This example is from VP-46 and is preparing to launch for a mission from Ali al Salem AB, Kuwait. *US Navy*

United States Marine Corps

Right from the start, it was clear that the US Marine Corps was to play a key role in Operation 'Iraqi Freedom'. The 15th Marine Expeditionary Unit (MEU) aboard the Tarawa Amphibious Ready Group arrived in the region in mid-February, followed by the 24th Marine Expeditionary Unit aboard the Nassau Amphibious Ready Group. The entire 1st Marine Division, with the 4th Amphibious Assault Battalion from Camp Pendleton, CA, 7th Marine Regiment and 3rd Battalion, were all deployed to Kuwait ready for action.

The 2nd Marine Regiment, Marine Aircraft Group 29 and the combat helicopters and Harriers deployed aboard the USS *Kearsarge* (LHD-3), USS *Bataan* (LHD-5), and the USS *Saipan* (LHA-2) completed the mighty Marines force. Ready to support troops on the ground were CH-46E Sea Knights, CH-53E Sea Stallions, UH-1N Hueys and AH-1W Cobras from MCAS New River as well as AV-8B Harriers from MCAS Cherry Point, NC. As well as the F/A-18 Hornet units embarked on the

Top: **A US Marine Corps AV-8B Plus of the 24th Marine Expeditionary Unit (MEU) blasts from the deck of the USS *Nassau* (LHA-4). The Harrier carries a GBU-12 LGB as well as the much-vaunted Litening II targeting pod.** *US Marine Corps*

Centre right: **The amphibious assault ships of Commander, Task Force Fifty One (CTF-51) come together in an unprecedented formation during operations in the North Arabian Gulf on 20 April. This marked the first time that six large deck amphibious ships from the East and West coasts had deployed together in one area of operation. Led by the flag ship USS *Tarawa* (LHA-1), the ships are (from left to right): USS *Bonhomme Richard* (LHD-6), USS *Kearsarge* (LHD-3), USS *Bataan* (LHD-5), USS *Saipan* (LHA-2), and USS *Boxer* (LHD-4). CTF-51 led US Navy amphibious forces in the Arabian Gulf region during OIF. The 32 ships of CTF-51 composed the largest amphibious force assembled since the Inchon landing, during the Korean War.** *US Navy*

Right: **The USS *Kearsarge* (LHD-3) on its way to the Gulf with elements of MAG-29 embarked. The ship was flagship for Amphibious Task Force East (ATF-E).** *US Navy*

US Navy carriers, squadrons also deployed to land bases in Kuwait. The US Marine Corps was ready for action.

As the land forces pushed deeper into Iraq they were supported by the heavy-lift CH-53s and medium-lift CH-46s, bringing in essential supplies and equipment. Ahead, Iraqi forces were being 'softened up' by the Cobras, Hornets and Harriers. It wasn't just here that the US Marine Corps presence was counting. Detachments of KC-130 Hercules tankers operated from Bahrain (VMGR-452) and Ali al Salem in Kuwait. At Prince Sultan AB (PSAB) in Saudi Arabia EA-6B Prowlers of VMAQ-1 also flew SEAD missions, clocking up an impressive 1,850 combat hours during 395 sorties over Iraq.

Top: **A US Marine Corps CH-53E Sea Stallion comes into the hover at 'Camp Coyote' in Kuwait as it prepares to lift a British Royal Marines vehicle.** *US Marine Corps*

Above: **US Marines of the 15th MEU enter a CH-46E aboard USS** *Tarawa* **(LHA-1) ready to transit into Kuwait to begin final preparations for the assault on Iraq.** *US Navy*

HARRIERS ATTACK

The US Marine Corps AV-8B Harrier IIs were in action from the outset, supporting operations in southern Iraq as Allied troops spilled over the border. OIF saw 76 US Marine Corps Harriers deployed to the Gulf – more than 40% of the 3rd Marine Air Wing's fixed-wing offensive firepower – which duly helped facilitate a rapid assault on Baghdad from the south. Around 60 of these AV-8Bs were sea-based aboard four 'Harrier carriers', while other examples from VMA-214 'Blacksheep' and VMA-542 'Flying Tigers' also flew from Ahmed Al Jaber in Kuwait.

The Harrier force went into OIF with a point to prove. Twelve years earlier during 'Desert Storm', 86 US Marine Corps day-attack AV-8Bs had flown 3,380 sorties and dropped nearly three million tons of ordnance, but at a price. No less than five aircraft were downed by the enemy, most falling victim to

Right: **The flight deck 'shooter' signals the launch of an AV-8B from the deck of USS** *Tarawa* **(LHA-1).** *US Navy*

MANPADS (Man-Portable Air Defence Systems). Post-war, the US Marine Corps set about broadening the aircraft's weapons suite and nocturnal capabilities, all of which resulted in the fielding of the AV-8B 'Night Attack' Harrier II, as well as the radar-equipped Harrier II Plus.

By the time the US Marine Corps was heading off for OIF, virtually all the standard 'day attack' AV-8Bs had been remanufactured as 'Night Attack' or radar-equipped jets. This allowed the seven frontline units to field 12 radar-equipped and four Night Attack variants per squadron. Further enhancing the Harrier's effectiveness in combat was the introduction of the Northrop Grumman AN/AAQ-28(V) Litening pod from 2001. This gave the force the ability to detect and attack targets using precision weapons and minimise collateral damage.

Once OIF started, Harriers began operations against the Iraqi Republican Guard's Baghdad and Al Nida Divisions, as part of 3rd MAW's overall campaign. The US Marine Corps performed this mission tasking so well that a contemporary Coalition 'battle hit assessment report' rated the Republican Guard divisions at less than 25% strength prior to a final ground attack by elements of the 1st Marine Division.

Commenting on the opening days of the war, the Commanding Officer of USS *Tarawa* (LHD-1), Capt Jay Bowling said; 'I'm impressed with how well these young men and women have been performing, especially under such tough circumstances and with so much at stake. They've done a great job supporting Harrier operations and the Marines ashore, as they push toward their next objective'.

Lt Col Lee Schram, AV-8B Harrier Co-ordinator at Marine Corps HQ in Washington, DC, added; 'The Harrier II force provided the Coalition with 24-hour Precision Strike, CAS, Armed and Aerial Reconnaissance assets during day, night and adverse weather conditions. It also provided operational

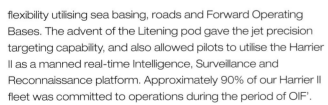

flexibility utilising sea basing, roads and Forward Operating Bases. The advent of the Litening pod gave the jet precision targeting capability, and also allowed pilots to utilise the Harrier II as a manned real-time Intelligence, Surveillance and Reconnaissance platform. Approximately 90% of our Harrier II fleet was committed to operations during the period of OIF'.

From 20 March through to 20 April 2003, the Harriers flew 2,182 sorties, enjoying a 79.3% average aircraft readiness rate. Some 79% of the ordnance dropped were precision-guided munitions with 478 targets destroyed by 375 tons of ordnance (887 precision-guided munitions and 198 freefall bombs). In stark contrast to 'Desert Storm', no Harrier IIs were damaged or lost to enemy fire.

Perhaps the final word on the Harrier II's employment in OIF should go to Lt Col Michael K. Hile, who was CO of VMA-311 'Tomcats'. Operating 18 jets split between two amphibious assault ships, it was the largest naval tactical aviation squadron supporting major combat operations in OIF; 'Soon after combat operations began, the Harrier II became the preferred aircraft for strikes because of its ability to confirm tactical-size

Top left: **Night one, AV-8Bs of VMA-214 'Blacksheep' prepare to launch from Al Jaber, Kuwait.** *US Marine Corps*

Above left: **A pair of US Marine Corps KC-130T Hercules of VMGR-234 'Rangers' transit the Iraq desert with the trailing aircraft punching out a salvo of decoy flares, designed to spoof enemy heat-seeking missiles.** *US Marine Corps*

Top right: **At sea with the Wasp-Class USS *Kearsarge* (LHD-3). In the background an AV-8B returns from a mission. The example in the foreground is an APG-65 radar-equipped AV-8B Plus.** *US Navy*

Above: **An AV-8B Plus of VMA-223 'Bulldogs' lands aboard USS *Kearsarge* (LHD-3) during OIF.** *US Navy*

targets from medium altitudes with its Litening pod. The success of the Harrier II in OIF was not due solely to the capabilities of the Litening pod, although it was the recognised difference in the Harrier II fleet today from other platforms. Many years of commitment by the Marine Corps has ensured that the Harrier II is a safe, reliable, relevant and sustainable aircraft, and that its pilots are effectively trained'.

Above: **Taxying in at its deployed base, VMFA-251 'Thunderbolts' sent Hornets to Al Jaber, Kuwait, from its home base at MCAS Beaufort, SC.** *US Navy*

HORNET STRIKES

US Marine Corps F/A-18 Hornets from the 2nd and 3rd Marine Aircraft Wing were deployed to Al Jaber in Kuwait as well as being embarked with US Navy air wings. In Kuwait, VMFA(AW)-121 'Green Knights', VMFA(AW)-225 'Vikings' and VMFA-232 'Red Devils' from MCAS Miramar, CA, joined VMFA-251 'Thunderbolts', VMFA(AW)–533 'Hawks' from MCAS Beaufort, SC.

Similar to the Harriers, the F/A-18s provided air support for ground forces, including the 1st Marine Division and British forces as they captured the port city of Umm Qasr before moving deeper into enemy territory.

According to Capt Jaden J. Kim, a Hornet weapons systems officer (WSO), with VMFA(AW)-121 'Green Knights', notable missions included Fast-Forward Air Control (Fast-FAC) and Close Air Support (CAS) missions to support the troops on the ground. 'Our squadron recently returned from Afghanistan and flew Operation 'Southern Watch' missions. We have experienced aircrews and our personnel knew the operational tempo would be high. We knew in the back of our minds the real importance of the missions. We were busy as we methodically and professionally did everything as we were trained to do, however, we realised there was an added sense of urgency because we knew the Marines on the ground were depending on us. It was phenomenal but strange to put bombs down range. It wasn't until after our return that it finally struck home that the 'game was on' and that was kind of shocking'.

Above: Turning and burning, a US Marine Corps CH-46E Sea Knight prapares to launch from USS *Kearsarge* (LHD-3). *US Navy*

Right: The workhorse of the US Marine Corps, the Sikorsky CH-53E Sea Stallion provides vital re-supply and transport capabilities for the Corps and was in action throughout OIF. *US Navy*

Below: High above Baghdad, this weathered F/A-18C is from VMFA-323 'Death Rattlers' embarked on the USS *Constellation* (CV-64) as part of CVW-2. *US Marine Corps*

Left: Returning to Al Jaber, Kuwait, after a night OIF mission on 21 March, is an F/A-18D of VMFA(AW)-225 'Vikings'. *US Navy*

Below left: 'Death Jesters' – a VMAQ-2 EA-6B Prowler departs Prince Sultan AB, Saudi, carrying ALQ-99 jamming pods. *USAF*

Above: **An AH-1W Cobra 'hot refuels' at a Forward Arming and Refuelling Point (FARP) in the opening days of OIF. The Cobras were busy supporting ground troops moving north towards Baghdad.**
US Marine Corps

COBRA BITE

Having been ferried to the region aboard the US Marine Corps amphibious assault ships, AH-1W Cobras and UH-1N Hueys started heading to shore bases ready to assault the Iraqi lines of defence. A total of 27 Cobras from HMLA-167 'Warriors' and HMLA-269 'Gun Runners' at MCAS New River, NC, operating as part of MAG-29 had deployed aboard USS *Kearsarge* (LHD-3), USS *Bataan* (LHD-5), and USS *Saipan* (LHA-2). A further 27 AH-1Ws deployed from MCAS Camp Pendleton, CA.

Once on the ground in Iraq, pilots soon realised that even the slightest wind stirred up a whirling 'brownout' of desert sand, making even the basics of flying hazardous. As ground forces prepared to head into Iraq, AH-1 Cobras were tasked with knocking out border posts and enemy positions nearby. As the troops moved forward, the Cobras also moved up supported by Forward Arming and Refuelling Points (FARPs). These were located in the most austere of locations, on highways, or just on scrub land. After refuelling and re-arming, the Cobras would typically shut down and assume a 'strip alert'. This meant that they could react quickly to support troops with CAS, all conducted in the extremely demanding desert conditions. Pilots experienced conditions like never before, flying in the pitch black, with swirling sand and little reference.

Crews rotated back and forth from the ships, flying missions out via FARPs as the war developed. The Cobras achieved significant success, hitting targets on the run with AGM-114 Hellfire missiles and 20mm cannon fire.

United States Army

As well as ground forces, the US Army had a massive aviation presence in the Gulf region for OIF, with around 136 AH-64 Apaches, OH-58 Kiowa Warriors and numerous other assets supporting the ground offensive. After Turkey rejected the use of its bases and airspace for military action, the US Army had to adapt to the situation. The 3rd Infantry Division (Mechanized) and V Corps launched a spearhead into Iraq from the south. Despite the NATO agreement on improved defences, Turkish-US relations failed to pave the way for US troops to deploy to the country for a possible invasion of Iraq from the north, with the US wanting to deploy the US Army's 4th Infantry Division in Turkey. The 4th Division eventually repositioned and followed the other units in from Kuwait.

As well as the headline-grabbing Apaches, the US Army's ubiquitous UH-60 Black Hawks provided vital battlefield utility roles including troop transport, re-supply and medical evacuation. The 101st Airborne Division (Air Assault) had three full battalions operating in northern Iraq. During the opening phases of OIF, Black Hawks from the 5-101 'Eagle Assault' spearheaded the 101st's assault on Baghdad. Although a number of UH-60s were, and have subsequently, been lost to enemy ground fire the type still provides unmatched air-mobility in combat.

Left: **OIF saw the 'Vipers' of the 1st Battalion (Attack), 3rd Aviation Regiment, debut the devastating AH-64D Longbow Apache in combat. Note this example's asymmetric loading of RF/SAL Hellfire missiles coupled with a single rocket pod and fuel tank.** *Maj David Rude/US Army*

Below: **A US Army UH-60 Black Hawk operates near Baghdad. The Black Hawk provided vital battlefield utility roles including troop transport, re-supply and medical evacuation during OIF.** *Department of Defense*

APACHES IN OIF

Like the AH-64A of 'Desert Storm' fame, Longbow Apaches of 1st Battalion (Attack), 3rd Aviation Regiment spearheaded the 3rd Infantry Division (Mechanized) assault into Iraq on 20 March 2003 in a combined attack aimed at destroying border observation posts and reconnaissance targets along the Kuwaiti-Iraqi border.

The largest Apache operation of the war was undertaken three nights later when 34 AH-64D Longbows from the 11th Aviation Brigade mounted a deep penetration raid to the outskirts of Karbala to engage the Republican Guard's Medina Division. Unexpectedly, the Apache force encountered intense enemy fire, coming under heavy attack from automatic weapons and RPGs (Rocket Propelled Grenades).

Although many of the Apaches involved were damaged, and one was downed and the crew captured, the enemy suffered heavy losses. Apache tactics evolved during the conflict, going from a stand-off, hovering fire platform, to a running fire mission, very similar to those conducted by AH-1 Cobra gunships in Vietnam.

Below: **A 'Viper' Apache on patrol near a Presidential Palace in Iraq.** *Maj David Rude/US Army*

Below left: **Soldiers of the 101st Airborne Division attach a sling load of food and water to a UH-60 Black Hawk.** *US Army*

Below right: **A 101st Airborne Division, 159th Aviation Brigade Medevac UH-60 Black Hawk lands at an austere strip near Mosul, Iraq.** *US Army*

Left: US Army helicopter crews conducted operations from austere strips, advancing with the troops to provide Close Air Support (CAS) around the clock. *Maj David Rude/US Army*

Below: During OIF, Apaches employed the deadly 30mm cannon, 2.75in rockets and both Radar Frequency (RF) and Semi-Active Laser (SAL) Hellfire III missiles. *Maj David Rude/US Army*

Left: The 'Vipers' of the 1st Battalion (Attack), 3rd Aviation Regiment were given markings that paid homage to its AH-1 Cobras of the Vietnam era, with all 18 of its AH-64Ds adorned with snakesmouths. *Maj David Rude/US Army*

Below left: Returning to the captured Iraqi base at Jalibah AB, a 'Viper' Apache completes another complex combat mission. The unit successfully flew over 850 combat hours in this extremely challenging environment with no combat losses. *Maj David Rude/US Army*

Bottom left: On patrol near the Tigris River, 'Viper' Apaches were always alert to threats on the ground. Iraqi forces adopted a tactic of placing a target in the open in an attempt to lure the Apache in for the kill. As the Apache set up its attack, an ambush was launched with mortar salvos by observers in civilian attire. *Maj David Rude/US Army*

Below: Half of the AH-64Ds of the 1st Battalion (Attack), 3rd Aviation Regiment were fitted with mast-mounted Fire Control Radar (FCR). The FCR aircraft would locate the targets, before relaying the targeting information to non-FCR aircraft. *Maj David Rude/US Army*

Right: En-route to another target in support of the US Army ground units, a 'Viper' Apache heads for action. Patrolling USAF E-8 J-STARS were able to datalink MTI (Moving Target Indicator) target information directly to the cockpit of the US Army's AH-64D Longbow Apache attack helicopters. *Maj David Rude/US Army*

1st Battalion (Attack), 3rd Aviation Regiment

OIF saw the 'Vipers' of the 1st Battalion (Attack), 3rd Aviation Regiment, debut the AH-64D Longbow Apache in combat. The battalion fired the first Radar Frequency (RF) Longbow Hellfire missile used in combat against observation posts along the Kuwaiti/Iraqi border – the first direct fire shots of the ground war – and obtained a direct hit, as did 13 other conventional missiles fired at this time.

The 'Vipers' also 'killed' the first Iraqi tank (a T-54) in the vicinity of Nasiriyah. It was in these early days of the conflict that the AH-64D was used in much the same way as the US Marine Corps use attack helicopters, in close combat attacks, or CCA, in support of ground forces. The 'Viper' battalion's Longbows destroyed everything they were tasked to destroy, conducted medical evacuation (MEDEVAC) escort and quick reaction force missions in support of ground units.

Unlike 'Desert Storm', Iraqi air defence units demonstrated adaptability and improvements in tactics, especially in their ability to target attack helicopters. The enemy placed weapon systems beneath tree lines and palm canopies, and they tucked them into urban areas to exploit the Apache's vulnerabilities. On more than one occasion, the enemy employed an obviously lucrative target, a T-55 or T-72 tank for example, in the open to act as bait with the expectation of drawing Apaches into an ambush. Observer teams located in the ambush positions (and wearing in Arab civilian attire) would then triangulate the Apaches' location and direct mortar and anti-aircraft artillery salvos upon them.

The 'Vipers' successfully flew over 850 combat hours in this extremely challenging environment with no combat losses. The unit's Apaches were given markings that paid homage to its AH-1 Cobras of the Vietnam era – as well as the unit's 'Viper' callsign, it had all 18 of its AH-64Ds adorned with snakesmouths in recognition of its Cobra ancestry.

Half of the battalion's Apaches were fitted with mast-mounted Fire Control Radar (FCR). The 'Vipers' used the FCR-equipped aircraft to scan the battlefield for targets, with crews then relaying digital targeting information to non-FCR equipped aircraft. The Apaches employed the deadly 30mm cannon, 2.75in rockets and both Radar Frequency (RF) and Semi-Active Laser (SAL) Hellfire III missiles.

Maj David Rude was Battalion Operations Officer for the 1st Battalion (Attack), 3rd Aviation Regiment during OIF; 'For much of OIF, I was in the 1st Battalion (Attack), 3rd Aviation Regiment's Tactical Command Post (TAC), controlling and resourcing the fight from the ground. My principal roles were to orchestrate the planning and execution of tactical missions, and to integrate our battalion into the overall fight in support of the 3rd Infantry Division (Mechanized). Our TAC, which was co-located with the Aviation Brigade TAC, conducted battle tracking of aircraft and units throughout the battlefield, and we provided a command and control node from the TAC on the ground, or from an airborne EH-60 Black Hawk command and control variant of the aircraft.

'The 18 AH-64D Longbow Apaches assigned to our battalion flew a myriad of attack, reconnaissance and security support missions during OIF. By the time we had reached Baghdad International Airport, our vehicles had accomplished a treacherous march that exceeded 400 miles across austere desert in the most challenging expeditionary warfare in contemporary history.

'One of the 'Vipers' most memorable actions occurred on 22 March. A team of two Apaches had completed a MEDEVAC escort mission west of Nasiriyah. As the AH-64Ds were returning to base at 'Objective Charlie' (Jalibah AB), they received an order to conduct a 'search and attack' mission to destroy two suspected Iraqi D-30 howitzers south of Tallil AB. Upon arriving at the search site, the leader received a distress call from an infantry officer on the ground. They were pinned down by heavy enemy fire, and had already taken several casualties. The 'Vipers' provided immediate fire support to shield the friendly vehicles from further Iraqi fire. Despite taking direct fire from the enemy, the Apaches continued their onslaught with decisive cannon, 2.75in rocket and Hellfires. Throughout the action, a soldier on the ground provided navigational reference calls and directed 25mm fire to orient the Apaches to the most critical enemy threat, three Anti-Tank Guided Missile (ATGM) systems'. As would be expected, the Apaches quickly neutralised the threat.

UNMANNED ARMY

The US Army's Northrop Grumman's RQ-5A Hunter unmanned aerial vehicles (UAVs) were deployed to Iraq in January 2003. The Hunter is tasked with collecting and relaying real-time reconnaissance, surveillance, and target-acquisition (RSTA) information, to ground control and mission monitoring stations. Originally intended to carry only sensor payloads, the Hunter has been modified to carry munitions, and demonstrated its ability to detect, track and monitor moving objects using an electro-optical/infrared sensor. Those deployed to Iraq were equipped with an extended centre wing that extends the UAV's endurance to more than 15 hours and provides it with the capability to deploy precision-guided weapons.

Overleaf: **The US Army worked tirelessly throughout OIF to ensure the swift outcome of the operation. Here a US Army UH-60 Black Hawk heads out to support troops at sundown.** *No 1(F) Squadron*

Operation 'Telic' The British War

RAF LEADS THE WAY

On 6 February, UK Defence Secretary Geoff Hoon announced a major commitment to possible military action against the Iraqi military regime. Given the name Operation 'Telic', the deployment involved around 100 Royal Air Force (RAF) fixed-wing assets and additional support from Joint Helicopter Command (JHC). The British presence in the Gulf region soon equated to around 42,000 personnel from all three services. Operation 'Telic' (derived from the Greek word for purposeful) also saw 1,200 Royal Marines from 3 Commando and 42 Commando deployed alongside 1,000 members of 16 Air Assault Brigade and components of the Army Air Corps.

Operation 'Telic' contributed a number of vital assets to the Coalition, such as Harrier GR7 and Tornado GR4/4A attack/recce aircraft, Tornado F3 air defence fighters, E-3D Sentry AWACS, Nimrod R1 ELINT platforms, recce Canberra PR9s, VC10 and TriStar tankers as well as JHC Pumas and Chinooks – all flying in an extremely demanding environment.

The RAF was extremely busy from the outset of Operation 'Telic'. The British strike force of Tornado GR4/4As and Harrier GR7s reported undertaking about six months' worth of flying in the brief period before the war to prepare for action. Prior to deploying, the Tornados were all fitted with 'hot and high'-rated RB199 Mk103 engines, new light grey radomes and a light grey Alkali Removable Temporary Finish (ARTF) overall paint scheme. The Tornados also received new hand controllers in the rear cockpit for the Defensive Aids Suite (DAS), which included the BOL-IR (Infra-Red) self-defensive Sidewinder missile rails.

As combat operations began, the RAF flew missions around the clock. Grp Capt Simon Dobb, Tornado detachment commander in Kuwait, said: 'We are expecting this to be on an unprecedented scale, far larger than Operation 'Desert Storm' in 1991'. On first night of the so-called 'Shock and Awe' Coalition attacks, Grp Capt Dobbs added that it was the 'greatest night in the history of the Tornado squadrons'. He went on to say that his detachment's attacks would be

Right: **Flying back to base after a strike mission, Tornado GR4 'Born Fighter' (ZA554/BF) and its flight leader prepare to recover to Al Udeid, Qatar.** *No 617 Squadron*

Below: **Heading into battle – Paveway II Laser-Guided Bomb-toting Tornado GR4s take on fuel from a No 101 Squadron VC10 K3 as they head into Iraq.** *No 12(B) Squadron*

'carefully targeted against the regime' and would 'minimise civilian casualties and infrastructure'.

From night one, Tornado GR4s from No IX(B) Squadron flew SEAD missions with the Air Launched Anti-Radiation Missile (ALARM) and attacked Iraqi radar defences as part of the massive air strikes on Baghdad. Grp Capt Dobb said: 'Our task is to take out the Integrated Air Defence Systems around Baghdad and thereby cause maximum isolation of Saddam Hussein's leadership and his infrastructures'. The RAF Tornado GR4/4A force also struck key Iraqi military targets around Al Kut and Kirkuk with the Enhanced Paveway laser/GPS-guided bomb. The Tornados also used the new Reconnaissance Airborne Pod for Tornado – RAPTOR. This provided essential Time-Sensitive Target (TST) information for air commanders, which has been seen as a vital role for the type to be fulfilling. Meanwhile, Harriers supported ground forces as well as striking key regime assets, and high above the battlefield the E-3s, Nimrods and Canberras provided additional eyes and ears for Coalition commanders.

TORNADO AT WAR

The RAF deployed a force of 32 Tornado GR4/4A ground attack aircraft to the Persian Gulf ready for the start of hostilities. From RAF Marham, Nos II(AC), IX(B) and 31 Squadrons deployed to the region, along with crews from No 13 Squadron. Two squadrons from RAF Lossiemouth, Nos 12(B) and 617 Squadron, also deployed to the Gulf, with the force making up two pooled Tornado Wings at Ali al Salem in Kuwait and at Al Udeid in Qatar. The Kuwait element was comprised mainly of Marham Wing assets, with No II(AC) Squadron, No IX(B) Squadron and No 31 Squadron, as well as six crews from Lossiemouth's No 617 Squadron. The latter crews were at Ali al Salem as it was the preferred location from which to undertake the new MBDA Storm Shadow attack mission. The crews were prepared for any scenario thanks to the phenomenal training they receive within the RAF – training that prepares these pilots and navigators to head off into the dead of night into a cauldron of dangers and challenges.

Left: The Royal Air Force deployed around 32 Tornado GR4/4As to the region under Operation 'Telic'. The GR4 has proved a highly potent tool for the RAF, with this example crewed by No IX(B) Squadron, operating from Ali al Salem, Kuwait. The squadron flew on the first night of the war and undertook the high-risk SEAD (Suppression of Enemy Air Defence) mission, employing the ALARM missile to tackle the Iraqi air defence network. *No IX(B) Squadron*

Below: The transit north into Iraqi airspace involved regular support from RAF VC10s. This GR4 crewed by No 617 Squadron 'Dambusters' carries a pair of Enhanced Paveway IIs. *No 617 Squadron*

Left: **The Combat Air Wing badge designed for the GR4/4A team at Ali al Salem, Kuwait, consisting of each unit's squadron badge.** *via No 12(B) Squadron*

Bottom: **Armed with a pair of MBDA Storm Shadows, a No 617 Squadron Tornado GR4 heads out for the first strike with the new Storm Shadow weapon.** *Crown Copyright*

'Dambusters' strike

The famous 'Dambusters' of No 617 Squadron were tasked with the operational debut of the new MBDA Storm Shadow stand-off, deep penetration cruise missile being used against high-value targets by the Tornado GR4. Crews from No 617 Squadron had prepared for the operational clearance of Storm Shadow and flew with the new weapon in the first few days of the war. Storm Shadow was rushed into service as part of a highly classified Urgent Operational Requirement (UOR) and reports from RAF sources say the weapon performed extremely well. The involvement of No 617 Squadron with this new missile was particularly significant as it coincided with the 60th anniversary of the squadron being formed to undertake the famous attacks on the Ruhr Dams under Operation 'Chastise' in WW2. At that time the unit pioneered the use of Barnes Wallis' Upkeep 'bouncing bomb' and the squadron again led the way with Storm Shadow.

'It was an historic mission for us', said Wg Cdr Dave Robertson, OC No 617 Squadron, as he spoke to reporters in Kuwait after the dramatic first mission. Having led the first Storm Shadow mission over Iraq on 21 March, Wg Cdr Robertson went on to describe how the sortie took the 'Dambusters' crews through heavy anti-aircraft fire. It transpired that one of his wingmen was forced to jettison fuel tanks in order to increase manoeuvrability as he was engaged by an Iraqi SAM.

Sqn Ldr David 'Noddy' Knowles and navigator Flt Lt Andy Turk were 'locked up' by an Iraqi SA-2 'Guideline' SAM as they prepared to attack targets to the north of Baghdad. Talking to reporters in the Gulf, Wg Cdr Robertson explained. 'Storm Shadows are heavy at 1,300kg each; Noddy and Andy were fuel critical so we let them go in first to fire their missiles. As we entered our attack run, we too came under missile attack'. Sqn Ldr Knowles and Flt Lt Turk were later awarded the DFC for their bravery during this mission (see also Foreword).

Wg Cdr Robertson and his pilot, Sqn Ldr Andy Myers, made use of the improved GR4 Defensive Aids Suite (DAS) and took evasive action before continuing on to deliver their two Storm Shadows. 'We were operating in a high-threat environment. Looking back I can say I was nervous. And I was excited, not in a joyful sense, but because I knew we were making history,' Robertson said at the time. 'I believe in what we are doing and I am confident that we are selecting regime targets using weapons that are accurate. I am proud of what we have achieved so far,' he added. Battle Damage Assessment showed the missiles hit their targets with pinpoint accuracy.

Above: **A No 12(B) Squadron Tornado GR4 navigator preps the jet as another mission gets underway. The green fabric cover helps to reduce glare on the left TV tab, which is used to display TIALD imagery.** *No 12(B) Squadron*

Flt Lt Andy Turk, No 617 Squadron

Flt Lt Andy Turk flew as a navigator on No 617 Squadron and he played a significant role in the introduction and employment of the Storm Shadow. 'My pilot and I flew 15 missions altogether and we generally took two or three GPS-guided Enhanced Paveway 1,000lb bombs or two Storm Shadow missiles. It may not sound like a lot of weapons, but if you hit something, as opposed to having a close miss, you only need one bomb to do the job.

'There's a lot of responsibility that turns into nerves just before an attack. I can only describe it as like the 'big match temperament'. It's the same kind of fear I imagine you'd get running out onto the pitch before an FA Cup final – making sure that when you kick off you don't fluff the first pass. Once you get into it you're fine. All the training you've done throughout your career, all the planning for a particular sortie effectively all

funnels down to a moment when you actually go and drop these bombs on a target.

'Avoiding civilian casualties is always going to be a big concern but at the end if the day you're a military person and you've just got to get on and do what you're tasked to do. The most significant worry I believe to all combatants out there was to avoid blue-on-blue or civilian casualties. We brought back weapons whenever targets were not positively identified (PID), we were in no doubt as to our responsibilities and Rules of Engagement.

'Our first mission (Storm Shadow) brought a sense of relief that all the work that our UK support assets and the squadron had put into getting a brand new system into operational use had come to successful fruition. We were confident of course that it would work, but you would be a fool not to consider the worst. We were focused on getting the job done and getting back safely. Our missiles were launched from locations close to Baghdad, thus we were targeted throughout the flight by SAMs and Triple-A. Additionally, the land battle below was intense. The sight of the start of the 'Shock and Awe' aspect of the campaign in Baghdad was unbelievable and we saw a hundred or so explosions in a space of the first minute or so. On one mission we saw what we thought was an explosion but then a bright dot came out of that explosion and followed us. As we banked right it corrected right and so on, and we soon realised it was a missile following our manoeuvres. We dumped our large fuel tanks so we could manoeuvre the aircraft a lot harder and banked hard right and then down and into the cloud. Our wingman saw an explosion a little way away from us. At the time you're completely focused on the task, but when the adrenaline has stopped pumping, that's when you realise how lucky you were'.

The crews of No 617 Squadron also dropped Paveway and 'dumb' bombs with total precision, as Flt Lt Turk explained: 'In those final seconds, when you have positively identified your target, and released the weapon, it's all down to you, there's nothing you can do to bring that bomb back. When you've

Below: **As night falls at Ali al Salem, Kuwait, the RAF Tornado GR4s are prepared for yet more strike missions. The GR4 and its highly professional crew can strike with deadly accuracy around the clock.** *Crown Copyright*

seen the explosion on target, you feel a sense of relief rather than jubilation. That's the point at which you think 'Ok, good, that has worked as I intended it to'. It's not a 'Yeeha, I've just broken their stuff or I've just killed a Republican Guard soldier.

'Supporting the land war was our primary task throughout the conflict. One evening we were tasked by a Forward Air Controller (FAC) to destroy artillery pieces in the outskirts of Baghdad that were engaging Coalition forces. The target area was heavily defended by Triple-A and we were targeted constantly throughout our attacks. The flashes from the Triple-A explosions made it very hard to be able to even see the TV display.

Above: **Preparing for the first Storm Shadow mission, a GR4 crew from No 617 Squadron check the weapon prior to departing Ali al Salem.** *Crown Copyright*

'Although the squadron had been actively involved with Storm Shadow concepts for the past two years, such as development of planning software and concept of operations, we only began flying with the aircraft software and mock weapon in late October 2002. The weapon does have a unique capability in its hard target penetration capabilities, but this was never going to be utilised until the system had been fully tested and proven. The final tasking was not released until we received our Air Tasking Order shortly prior to onset of operations over Iraq. The trials were initiated by BAE Systems then continued by the Strike Attack OEU (SAOEU). No 617 Squadron was due to participate in the trials but events in the Gulf overtook us. The SAOEU continued the trials as we deployed to the Gulf.

'The jets required only minor modifications for Storm Shadow, generally related to the Stores Management System and a new version of aircraft's software, which took a relatively short time to do. This allowed us to use the aircraft in other roles such as the LGB or recce when not required for Storm Shadow.

'For the Storm Shadow missions we generally flew four-ship formations, which split into pairs for the attacks. We employed our standard medium-level tactics. The missile can be programmed with different mission options. These options can then be selected in-flight the giving flexibility to vary the target or missile routing. The 'Telic' missiles were fired on specific targets; we would not need to re-programme them post-launch. We employed the weapon against high-value targets that needed a penetrating weapon and high degree of accuracy'.

Right: **Strike a pose** – a GR4 navigator from No IX(B) Squadron takes a moment out during a mission to snap a self portrait. Like other Coalition flyers, some Tornado GR4 crews wore helmets with laser eye protection visors due to concerns over ground lasers used by Iraqi forces. No IX(B) Squadron

Flt Lt Dave Bolsover, No 617 Sqn

'One particular pre-targeted mission was a classic air interdiction mission rather than the CAS we did later on. In this particular case it was a Scud storage and maintenance facility well west of Baghdad. It involved planning the mission for about four hours. This saw us getting the co-ordinates, having an initial brief by the mission planner on what we were going to do, going from the mission planning side, putting the sortie together, then a mission briefing, followed by an out-briefing where the intelligence picture was updated and the ground troop positions updated – only then were we ready to go. We then walked to the aeroplane, started up and, from our position, it was typically just over an hour's transit to get to a tanker. It could be a VC10, TriStar, a USAF KC-135 or KC-10. After tanking we got the four-ship together and pushed for the target. We ran in just as dawn broke. We dropped the weapons and then came off the target. There was some SAM activity so our accompanying F-16CJs were firing HARMs as we were coming off the target'.

The massive effort to avoid 'blue-on-blue' and civilian casualties resulted in a number of types conducting Strike Co-ordinating Armed Reconnaissance (SCAR) missions. SCAR builds on the traditional FAC-A role and involves getting the attack aircraft onto the correct target in a 'Kill Box'. Platforms such as the F/A-18F Super Hornet and the F-15E Strike Eagle regularly set up CAP on station over a particular Kill Box and

used information from Intelligence, Surveillance and Reconnaissance (ISR) platforms as well as onboard systems to detect Iraqi military targets and identify them with onboard FLIR systems to confirm them as being hostile through PID (Positive Identification). The US Litening pods proved particularly effective in this role, though the three Advanced Targeting FLIR (ATFLIR) pods in theatre for the Super Hornets reportedly proved unreliable.

Flt Lt Bolsover recalls one such SCAR mission. 'Most of the later missions were CAS, with the theme being to go to the tanker and then head for a Kill Box. We would then be given targets either by SCAR or by a FAC. The TIALD pod on the GR4 is good but you need a pod with a resolution good enough to be able to carry out a PID and also collateral damage estimates of the target before you can drop on it. If someone is saying to you, 'you can drop on this target if you PID it' then you need something that can achieve this. This can be done with TIALD but it can be difficult'.

Below: **The No 617 Squadron 'Dambusters' detachment at Ali al Salem photographed on the squadron's 60th anniversary as it prepared for operations over Iraq in March.** Crown Copyright

Above: Prior to deploying to the Gulf, RAF Tornado GR4s received a number of minor defensive aids modifications as well as new overall light grey ARTF (Alkali Removable Temporary Finish) paint and light grey nosecones. *No 617 Squadron*

Left: Heading north into Iraq as the sun sets, the GR4 crew prepares to don Night Vision Goggles (NVGs) for a night strike. *No 12(B) Squadron*

Below: The busy flightline at Al Udeid. The base was home to RAF Tornado GR4s as well as the Royal Australian AF Hornets and the USAF's 379th AEW. *No 12(B) Squadron*

Left: **As well as RAF and USAF tanker assets, the US Marine Corps KC-130s operating out of Ali al Salem, Kuwait, and Sheikh Isa, Bahrain, supported RAF fast jets.** *No 617 Squadron*

Below left: **An RAF Tornado GR4 plugs into a VC10 and takes on fuel. Its crew is shown wearing NVG-compatible helmets, which don't have dark visors – so sunglasses are the order of the day before night sets in.** *No 617 Squadron*

OUT-FOXING IRAQ
Wg Cdr Mark Roberts,
OC No 12(B) Squadron

Wg Cdr Mark Roberts flew in the first Gulf War and this time was leading his squadron into combat. 'On one particular mission we were basically going in to fly CAS (Close Air Support) for ground troops in the Baghdad area. After holding for a while and not receiving any targets we were told to head for Tikrit because there was a target on the MSR (Main Supply Route). We were in contact with a number of agencies including AWACS and some ground co-ordination teams. The AWACS then got us onto the same frequency as a USAF Predator UAV that was flying in that area. Amazingly the Predator operator was actually remote from the theatre of operations and he talked my navigator's eyes onto the target. This was done through the TV-tab display in the back and was being done at night using infra-red. We ran in and attempted an attack, which didn't work out for a variety

Right: **Wg Cdr Mark Roberts, Officer Commanding No 12(B) Squadron, proudly shows off a Union Jack flag flown over Baghdad in his GR4 on a mission on 1 April 2003, the 85th Anniversary of the RAF.** *No 12(B) Squadron*

Below: **The Tornado GR4 detachment at Al Udeid, Qatar.** *No 12(B) Squadron*

of different reasons, then came back round. We were now very short of fuel and so we had to get the attack done quickly and after a very rapid liaison between ourselves and the Predator operator it was evident that he could actually help us mark the target. This was exactly what he did. We ran in, dropped the weapon and destroyed the target. What I think is incredible about the story is the fact that it was obviously a complete Coalition effort by a UK Tornado and an American Predator, whose operator was remote from the theatre of operations.

'One of our biggest strengths is that we train to be fully flexible – every part of the training syllabus has an element of flexibility in it. The people are expected to think, use common sense and apply a raw knowledge. So rather than strictly adhering to particular weapon profiles or a particular way of flying the aeroplane, what they will do is expand their

knowledge. With flexibility and common sense you can pretty much do or make anything work. That is where we have a tremendous amount of strength. That is not to say we are not disciplined, indeed we have a great reputation for this, particularly in the Iraqi theatre and certainly for the 10-12 years between the wars. We have earned an enormous amount of respect for our accuracy and discipline – and that is largely because if there is any doubt in the crews minds they don't drop. This actually makes us very valuable for the senior commanders because they know we strictly adhere to the collateral damage considerations, something that has an overriding importance.

'In terms of flexibility it was exactly the same in first Gulf War. Back then we arrived expecting to do the whole thing at low-level. When we went to medium-level it was a completely new skill for the Tornado'. Expanding on the differences between the two wars, Wg Cdr Roberts said; 'In the first Gulf War, I was a junior pilot on No 16 Squadron at Tabuk. This time round my role was completely different. It was a different personal challenge – an immense challenge – but nevertheless good to take on. In terms of the operation, I think the main difference was that last time we knew that we would be flying through the threats. We knew that at low-level in particular we would be flying through Triple-A. One interesting thing I discovered in the previous war is that it doesn't matter how long a conflict is, or where it is, or who it involves – it takes exactly the same amount of courage for the crews to get airborne, go and do the job repeatedly as it does in any conflict'. Indeed, such

Above: **A GR4 takes on fuel from a USAF KC-135R. Some of the 'Truffle Snuffler's' missions lasted over seven hours with numerous trips up to the tanker to replenish fuel tanks.** *No IX(B) Squadron*

courage was certainly ever-present in striking deep into Iraqi territory once again. Wg Cdr Roberts continued; 'This time you didn't really know where the threat was going to be and I think in that respect this campaign was a little more unpredictable. Certainly the instances where people had close calls with AAA and SAM activity often came as a surprise as it wasn't always in an area where we were expecting it. We had a couple of SAM missiles that got fairly close. I was flying with my navigator Sqn Ldr John Turner on a CAS mission in the hold waiting to be given a target just the South of Baghdad. Over the years I have seen a lot of Triple-A but we had about five rounds burst very close to the aeroplane. It was so close that you could see the gas ball expand and see the shrapnel around the edge of the gas ball, which I haven't ever seen before. Then just as that happened we saw a relatively large (SAM) missile go past us and again it was close enough that you could see the propellant spitting out the back. We looked above to see two aircraft evading, I think they were F-16s but it was a bit difficult to tell at night. That sort of thing was going on all the time and people felt threatened'.

As well as being a great medium-level precision strike platform, the GR4 was optimised for the low-level attack profile. The RAF maintains its low-level skills as it is a vital capability that may be called upon at any time, as Wg Cdr

Roberts explained. 'If the troops on the ground had been in contact and the weather was poor, we would have needed to get CAS to them. We would have needed to get our eyes onto the target, as in true CAS where you are really close to an enemy that's right up to the front edge of your own troops. If that had happened to us we would have gone low-level. It did happen in some cases because there were people flying low-level – the American A-10s in particular. There is no way that you can easily convert somebody who is used to the medium-level regime to low-level, but going the other way it is very straight forward because being competent at low-level gives you competence everywhere really. There was some low-level done in the western desert by the Tornado crews (see later), and we were prepared to go low-level if necessary – we were trained and ready to go for it'. Further asserting the combat attributes of the GR4, Wg Cdr Roberts added; 'The whole aeroplane is now beautifully optimised for night low-level operations and had we needed to do it we would have done, absolutely no question'.

Sqn Ldr 'D-L', No 12(B) Squadron

'On the first night we wanted all our kit working, so the jets had to be in top condition,' Squadron Leader 'D-L' explained. 'We generally flew as three or four ships, and employed everything from 'Legacy' Paveway II/III, ALARM, RBL755 and Enhanced Paveway II/III. When the US Army V Corps advanced on Baghdad we were at our busiest, with the Coalition flying up to 1,000 sorties a day to degrade the three Republican Guard Divisions to the south of the city.

During the air campaign, Iraq was divided up into a series of zones known as 'Kill Boxes' that were then used as areas of responsibility for aircrews. 'We received our pre-flight tasking from the CAOC. Our Wing 'Warlord' would then come across and brief us about five hours prior to take-off. If we were doing CAS, we'd be told our Kill Box and then go off and plan the sortie.

'We also flew SEAD (Suppression of Enemy Air Defence) missions and these would normally be made up of mixed assets. For example we'd be working with the EA-6B Prowlers and we did quite a lot with the F-16CJs that were based alongside us – particularly in the early days when we were going into Baghdad. They would perform a SEAD sweep ahead of us. We also undertook a number of missions with No IX(B) Squadron – there were always people you could call on.

The Tornado GR4s were using the new Enhanced Paveway GPS/laser-guided bombs to great effect. 'On one of our missions along the banks of the Saddam Canal, they (Coalition ground troops) were coming under heavy fire from three Iraqi tanks on the other side of the river. They basically asked 'can you bomb this position? Here are the co-ordinates'. We radioed back 'yes, got that position, looks like it is on the north side of the Saddam Canal'. They came back 'Yes that's good, go for it', and we did'.

But not all targets were so easily identified. 'We were desperate to avoid collateral damage,' 'D-L' explained. 'We were given a target one night in the north, and they said 'look, it is a military convoy we need you to go over there and bomb it'. We asked them to confirm that it was military, but they said 'no you need to PID (Positive Identify) it'. We couldn't. We could see a convoy, we could see people. We even dropped from

20,000ft to 15,000ft to see if the TIALD (Thermal Imaging and Airborne Laser Designator) pod could get a better picture. My navigator 'JJ' said, 'I still can't say whether or not that is military', so we brought the bombs back that night'.

No 12(B) Squadron flew a number of missions that included SCAR. 'We had some good SCAR. We had four (F-14A) Tomcats based with us. They were good because they could pass target data to us when we pitched up. There were some frustrations during missions over Baghdad though. A couple of the targets we were crying out to be identified, but some of the SCAR and FAC wasn't working very well and we ended up having to come back. That was our decision because we weren't happy with the target, the target information was taking too long'.

Sqn Ldr Simon Tickle, No 12(B) Squadron

'I flew eight missions over Iraq, seven at night and one daytime. Generally I flew as a pairs leader with TIALD and a pair of Enhanced Paveway IIs (EPW2). My number two generally carried three EPWs or four RBL755s, which gave us a flexible load out. We generally started preparing five hours before the mission. This started with a met' brief, intelligence brief, electronic warfare overview and an update from the squadron GLO (Ground Liaison Officer) to give us the situation on the ground. We then met up with the Warlord, a Squadron Leader from Lossie who liased with the CAOC (Combined Air Operations Centre) to get our tasking. Generally we were tasked to a 'Kill Box' or a target set. This usually involved Republican Guard, Iraqi armour or artillery, as well as a secondary target. We generally got airborne and headed straight up the 'Parkway' towards Iraq. The tanker was our next step and we initially contacted these in tracks over Saudi, however, the tanker tracks soon pushed over the border into Iraq in a bid to get them nearer to the action'.

Photos: No 12(B) Squadron

THE 'TRUFFLE SNUFFLERS'

During the build up to hostilities in early 2003, President Bush declared that one of his highest priorities would be to prevent attacks by Iraqi Scud missiles. In order to combat the Scud threat (already proven in the 1991 Gulf War), a significant force was allocated to the western desert of Iraq to search for and destroy any such systems. On the ground, this force was made up of Coalition Special Forces, whilst in the air the area would be under surveillance around the clock from E-3 AWACS, USAF J-STARS, RAF Canberra PR9s and US RQ-1 Predator UAVs. Strike assets assigned to tackling the threat were USAF B-1B Lancers, F-15s, F-16s, A-10s and RAF Harrier GR7s. Initially, the plan hinged on medium-level coverage and Precision Guided Munitions attacks, laser designated from the finding platform, or in co-operation with other aerial assets. But, as the conflict drew closer, it became apparent that weather conditions would preclude the medium-level search on some occasions. As a result, a limited number of the low-level-specialised RAF Tornado GR4A crews from Nos II(AC) and No XIII Squadrons joined the programme in mid-December 2002.

The counter-Scud plan had been developing over the months leading up to this point, and two practice exercises had been conducted (each one building on the level of complexity). On 2 January 2003, the crews from RAF Marham deployed to Nellis AFB, NV, amidst the highest secrecy to participate in a mission rehearsal should conflict become necessary. This is an account of No II(AC) Squadron's involvement in this very important Time Sensitive Targeting (TST) programme, from the mission rehearsal through to the conflict itself.

Below: **Armed and dangerous – a Tornado GR4A at Ali al Salem is readied for a TST mission over the western desert of Iraq.**
No IX(B) Squadron

Training for war

'On 2 January 2003, two of our GR4s were trailed out to Nellis AFB, along with the Harrier GR7 contingent from No 3 Squadron. The mission rehearsal took over the 'Red Flag' building, and No II(AC) Squadron operated out of here. Before flying began, CENTCOM commander General Tommy Franks addressed the participants and stressed the importance of the mission. The threat of the use of Weapons of Mass Destruction was very real.

'Due to the concentrated nature of the rehearsal, and the fact that the Tornado crews were very much the new faces, the decision was made to limit the flying to just two crews, with the other crew acting in a mission planning and support

Above: **The special weapons fit for the 'Truffle Snufflers' included TIALD laser designator pod and three retarded 1,000lb 'dumb' bombs.** *Sqn Ldr Gale*

capacity. Each mission was run in a similar way to a 'Red Flag' exercise and an attempt was made to transport the western Iraqi desert to Nevada! This was achieved by using the same 'Kill Box' grid system to describe locations that would be used in the conflict, and by nominating specific 'named areas of interest' in the Nevada desert, where it was thought the Scuds and their support equipment were most likely to be. Real Scuds and support equipment were released to roam the desert in accordance with instructions from the mission director – the Scud hunt, Nevada style, was on.

'The entire exercise was conducted at night, as this was assessed as the most likely time that the Scuds would venture out of their hides. The first challenge was to convince the Tornado that it wanted to air-to-air refuel behind a USAF KC-10 tanker at 25,000ft as the aircraft is not blessed with much excess power at that altitude. Other jets on the wing found it most amusing to see the GR4 plugged in taking fuel at the front, and throwing it out the back, in the shape of full afterburner on one engine!

'Initially, it was difficult for the Tornado to get any tasking orders, the weather was good and the medium-level search plan worked well. Luckily, the weather turned bad mid-week and the low-level Tornado came to the fore. We prosecuted several successful seek and destroy tasks in concert with a B-1B Lancer. Mainly as a result of the successes of this one mission, backed up by a further successful performance the following night, the Tornados were officially 'dealt in' to the counter-Scud gameplan. Following the exercise, the team remained at Nellis for a further week to work with the Scud targets on the Nellis ranges in order to continue the development of attack procedures and to work up all the aircrew that had not flown on the live-fly the week before.

'The Tornado TST team was expanded to include seven crews. Throughout February, flying exclusively at night and at low-level, the team practised procedures and techniques against an inflatable tank mounted on the back of a flat bed truck, which was driven around Sculthorpe airfield, Norfolk, and

Above: The Tornado GR4 and its aircrews again proved extremely versatile and effective during Operation 'Telic'. *No 617 Squadron*

Right: Tornado GR4A ZG714/Q sported particularly fitting nose art 'Truffle Snufflers' and 'It's a Recce Thang' – applied by the groundcrew at Ali al Salem during the conflict. *Sqn Ldr Gale*

the surrounding countryside. Along with Sqn Ldr 'Windy' Gale, who acted the part of AWACS, there were many ground teams, ATC personnel and airborne assets all involved. By using this set up, a GPS and a mobile phone, it was found to be possible to task the aircraft to 'investigate' in the vicinity of the inflatable even while it was on the move.

'The planned loadout for the aircraft was one that had never been tried before. A TIALD targeting pod was used to look ahead of the aircraft and locate targets some miles in front. To destroy them, either 1,000lb high-drag dumb bombs or cluster weapons were to be used. This presented several problems; firstly, these aircraft configurations had never been flown before and would need approval. In addition, the use of a precision laser designation pod (optimised for high-level attacks) to slave the weapons system in order to conduct a low-level non-precision weapon delivery, was untried, and when it was practised, produced bomb scores some 300ft long. This was overcome by using both the TIALD pod and the aircraft's own laser for attacks and the team was declared combat ready in mid-February. Under the leadership of Sqn Ldr Gale, the all-new strike package departed to the Gulf on 28 February'.

In theatre

'After a short period of settling in, and flying regular 'Resinate South' missions (which included a 'Response Option' against a Roland SAM located at H2 airfield in the western desert), final preparations for war began. Unfortunately, the new weapon configuration clearances were not forthcoming in time and verbal clearance was subsequently obtained from HQ. One change in the tactics was the decision not to carry cluster weapons for fear of harming Coalition forces. We also needed approval for the Tornados to operate at low-level, high-risk, missions when required and this was duly authorised both by the UK air component commander, Air Marshal Burridge and by US Generals Franks and Moseley.

'At Ali Al Salem, crews from across the Tornado Wing at Marham, along with crews from No 617 Squadron at Lossiemouth, amalgamated to form the 'Combat Air Wing' (CAW) under the leadership of Officer Commanding No 31

Squadron, Wg Cdr Paddy Teakle. The TST team became known variously as 'The Tufty Club' and the 'Truffle Snufflers', referring to the fact that they would be the only fast jets operating at low-level during the war as they attempted to 'sniff out' the Scuds. Away from the Scud campaign, No II(AC) Squadron crews would be allocated within CAW formations where required. As 'D-day' approached, the weather turned poor, and it was clear that the Tornados would be involved in the first combat missions of Operation 'Telic'. With 'D-day' originally planned for 19 March, followed by 'A-day' on the 21st, we were going to fly our first TST mission on 20 March'.

The following is from Sqn Ldr Gale's diary from the night of the first mission:

Thursday 20 March

'The big day. Some air attacks and cruise missiles went in last night so things had well and truly kicked off by the morning. I took two temazepam last thing to send me off to sleep. I have been doing this for a while on our wacky hours. They are really effective – yesterday, my watch was on its second go when it woke me up.

'Today I slept right through it and was woken up by 'Dave' shaking my arm to tell me that there had been two air attacks already and he thought a third was just starting. From our accommodation you could hear the tannoy, which always broadcasts first and they were saying 'air attack red' followed closely by our own tannoys; 'Scud attack, air attack red'. On with the gas mask and down into the 'Snakepit' bomb shelter.

'All this ate into our planning time for our sortie that afternoon and night, so it was doubly chafing when we stuck our heads out of the shelter after the 'all clear' to get another air attack minutes later. We finally escaped the shelter to get into work almost an hour and a half late, to try and decode an ATO (Air Tasking Order) that had been corrupted during transfer and didn't really have many left details on it. Luckily we had been highly focussed and had planned this sortie over the last couple of days. We had another air attack while at work, and instead of running to the shelter where there wasn't enough room, we decided to mask and suit up in the 'Tufty' room with the air conditioning off. It was better than being stuck outside and it's inside a blast wall. The bottom line is that we needed to keep working through air attacks and not scuttle off as we had important things to do.

'We managed to get some nosebag, 'Marcus' got us some sandwiches, and once we'd had our intelligence and met briefs, we had no time to do anything but outbrief, get in the bus and go – it wasn't supposed to be like this! All our plans for a measured brief, music choice in the bus, etc, gone!

'The manic rush made things easier in some ways, as we didn't have much time to dwell on what we were about to do and get nervous, but also, the lack of any time for final preparations made us all apprehensive.

'In the outbrief, we got the words that General Moseley had approved our plan to go low-level, and we were cleared into the operating areas – it had all come together. When we got to

the jet, we had time for a couple of photos, and my wife's teddy bear made an appearance in the cockpit!

'Doing the walkround was unreal. The jet really was loaded with TIALD, a guider of precision weapons, and three retarded 1,000lb 'dumb' bombs! When we took off, it was the first time the Tornado had ever flown in this configuration and it gave me a huge sense of satisfaction.

'It was broad daylight when we went and we flew on out into a setting sun. We finally managed to raise an AWACS and got the tanker frequency. It had taken about an hour to get to our tanker, an RAF TriStar. Because we had got off slightly late, and there had been a strong headwind, we were almost 20min late in joining for the refuel. This meant that 'Bill' and 'Dan' actually got in ahead of us, which was no problem, as we had now decided to miss out the first few targets, and start at batch two. By doing this, we made the conscious decision to run ourselves below the fuel that we needed to get back to Ali al Salem so were now working the divert to Arar in Saudi. This seemed sensible, as we joined with the tanker, but turned sour when I plugged in and no fuel flowed. I withdrew and re-plugged, no flow. The guys in the tanker recycled their switches, no flow. Withdrew and recycled my probe, replugged, fuel flows. Phew! We tanked up until he said we could have no more – this was significantly below what we really needed and was because at that time the radio was buzzing with talk of a helicopter crash and the launch of a CSAR mission. This wasn't a good start and was pretty sobering'.

Going in...

'We didn't have enough fuel or time to do our first set of targets, so we pushed in at medium-level. About this time 'Dan' called up to say he a problem and was RTB (returning to base). It turns out his TIALD had totally failed, which was real bad luck, but not for us, as we would be the first to go low-level over Iraq in a fast jet since 1991! We went back to the tanker, who was

Right: Flying night low-level missions using Night Vision Goggles (NVGs) is extremely demanding. These low-level, high-risk, missions were entrusted to the expert crews of Nos II(AC) and XIII Squadrons. *Sqn Ldr Gale*

Right: **A pair of RAF Tornado GR4s punch out decoy flares from the BOZ countermeasures pod.** *Lou Drummond*

now able to give us the full offload and fill us to the brim. This time there was no going back.

'We pushed in at medium-level and let down using the TFR (terrain following radar) in an area of nothingness. It was totally dark as the moon hadn't risen and there was absolutely nothing on the ground. It was impossible to fly visually, so the TF took the strain.

'We were tasked with checking out under two bridges on this section. We found the first and checked it was clear (the roads were really busy which was very surprising), then moved on to the second. Unbelievably, especially when you consider just how many of these things Iraq has, 'Dave' yelped that he could see something in this dark culvert under the road. We couldn't PID it, but he said there was definitely something there, and he could see a cab of some sort. I quickly called up the AWACS. It felt kind of unbelievable that this really could be it.

'We spun round a couple of times and further described this event to all the players. We explained that you couldn't see it from medium-level and strongly suggested that they send in a ground team to check it out. We then had to go back to the tanker to refuel. When I plugged this time, we lost all pressurisation! Things then got pretty cold, but we got our fuel and went back on task.

'This time low-level was pretty noisy, as the canopy seal was deflated, and we lost the radar due to no cooling from the air conditioning! We further chatted to AWACS and they tasked us to investigate the site again. We flew over and this time, it was obvious that whatever it was had reversed further back under the bridge. We passed this on. Pretty soon after, the lack of cooling got to our RHWR (Radar Homing and Warning Receiver) and we decided that discretion was the better part of valour as we now had no means of detecting whether enemy radars were looking at us.

'We went back to the tanker to wait for 'Gary' and 'Apples', but they didn't arrive so we set sail home. It was a hugely tedious hour home. I had a minging headache from not having drunk any water for 10hrs and I was looking forward to landing. We got comms with 'Gary' eventually – it turned out that they had taken off, had multiple failures, landed and taken another jet! Good skills chaps.

'I was desperate to land, so imagine my delight when Ali al Salem had another air raid when I was 10 miles out with the gear down and ready to get back to earth! We overshot and held off on the Saudi border until the alert was over then rushed back in to land. On touchdown, the right thrust reverser failed so some quick override selections later and a hefty stomp on the brakes, and the world started to slow down again! Time at last to relax.

'The sortie had lasted five minutes shy of seven hours. We signed the jet in and headed back to ops... just in time for another air raid. Once this was over, we got a chance to look at the video. It hadn't run to start with, but 'Dave' had taken it out on the second tanker bracket and given it some violence to encourage it, so we had coverage of the last pass.

'You could definitely see that there was something there under the bridge, but it was impossible to say what. I called this in to the CAOC, to make sure that someone was checking it out. Wg Cdr 'J-L' was on shift and was over the moon; yes,

there had been something there, J-STARS had seen something moving out from under the bridge after we had gone, and some F-16s had been tasked to investigate it but had lost it. He was ecstatic that we had found it with no help from anyone, not bombed it, so had acted in accordance with the ROE (Rules of Engagement – we couldn't positively identify and there were lots of civilian coaches travelling over the bridge) and that we had handed it off so effectively. Really, really happy, but obviously it would have been nice to bash that puppy! All in all, it couldn't have gone much better for us on the first night. I think we took them totally by surprise'.

The reality of war

'On Sunday 23 March we received the worst possible news. Kev Main and Dave Williams had been shot down and killed by a Patriot missile whilst on recovery to Ali at about 02.00hrs. This 'friendly fire' incident was a bitter pill to swallow so early in the conflict. It was essential to try to continue as normal, although we all knew that this could have happened to any of us.

'Several long nights of TST missions ensued. On Monday 24 March, I was woken up by yet another air raid. After a number of technical problems I got airborne but the weather was dreadful and the autopilot wouldn't work in TF so it was hours of manual e-scope, backed up with the FLIR (Forward-Looking Infra-Red). This was followed by some nightmare tanking in thickish cloud. I took ages to get in and the basket seemed to be sliding the wrong way! Having got in, the burner blew out after a couple of minutes. Following that, I got in, but with too much overtake, so throttled back and went up again. Unfortunately, the engine didn't come quickly enough and we slid majestically off the basket! Worst trouble I've ever had getting in to a tanker in my life.

'It was funny to fly over H2 on this night. We were there a few weeks ago at 20,000ft, bombing the Roland missile and now we're right down whistling past their ears! We saw some muzzle flashes on the ground, but no more'.

These missions were some of the most demanding and high-risk throughout the campaign. The above account highlights the level of professionalism, skill and bravery of the aircrews and the ability to adapt to requirements as they materialise, no matter how challenging.

HARRIERS ATTACK

The RAF swiftly deployed Harrier GR7s from Nos 1(F), 3(F) and IV(AC) Squadron to the region. Nine jets from No 3(F) Squadron formed 'Det A' at Azraq, Jordan, led by Wg Cdr Stuart Atha and Wg Cdr Rob Adlam, who assumed the role of base commander at the location. The Harriers arrived on 9 March and flew several hundred missions over Iraq supporting operations in the western desert.

The remaining two Harrier squadrons from Cottesmore, Nos 1(F) and IV(AC) Squadrons, made up 'Det B' at Ahmed Al Jaber in Kuwait. Initial combat missions saw the Harriers tackling strategic targets, but the majority of the war saw them providing Close Air Support (CAS) for troops on the ground, employing the full-spectrum of weapons including laser-guided Paveway II, GPS-guided Enhanced Paveway II (E-Paveway) and AGM-65G2 Maverick missiles to attack tanks, Surface-to-Surface Missiles (SSMs), Armoured Personnel Carriers (APCs), storage facilities, artillery pieces, Surface-to-Air Missiles (SAMs), Ba'ath Party HQs and even 'a couple of ships'!

Flt Lt Paul Francis was a Junior Pilot on No 1(F) Squadron at the time of deployment, and had been declared as being combat ready just days before flying to Kuwait. 'I flew mainly CAS missions and 'Kill Box' Interdiction. We used image-stabilised binoculars to PID targets from altitude. We worked heavily with US Marine Corps Ground Forward Air Controllers (GFACs) and also with USAF F-15Es who provided SCAR. Some missions would involve us getting airborne with E-Paveway to attack a pre-planned target, but many of our missions involved us getting tasked once we were airborne'.

Towards the end of the air war the Harriers operated with the Electro-Optic GP1 reconnaissance pod loaned from the Jaguar Force to search for any remaining pockets of resistance. This drew some impressive results, with the imagery being quickly exploited by the CAOC.

Top left: High above Iraq, a Harrier GR7 flown by a No 1(F) Squadron pilot heads towards its target. The Harrier carries a pair of Enhanced Paveway II (EPW2) bombs on the inner wing pylons. *No 1(F) Squadron*

Top: Heavy load. The RAF Harrier detachment at Ahmed al Jaber, Kuwait, was manned by personnel from Nos 1(F) and IV(AC) Squadrons. *Crown Copyright*

Above: Wearing an NVG-compatible helmet, an RAF Harrier pilot crews in for a night strike mission. *Crown Copyright*

Left: RAF Harriers worked as pairs or four-ships, tackling targets inside Iraq with precision accuracy. *No 1(F) Squadron*

Above: Taking on fuel from a USAF KC-10A Extender, this sharkmouthed Harrier GR7 is equipped with a pair of Legacy Paveway II Laser-Guided Bombs (LGBs) and a TIALD (Thermal Imaging and Airborne Laser Designator) pod. *via No 1(F) Squadron*

Right: The first few days of the war saw numerous chemical weapons alerts as Iraq fired crude missiles into Kuwait. This forced squadron personnel to abandon tasks at hand, don protective suits and sprint for shelter. *No 1(F) Squadron*

Below: The Harrier enclave at Al Jaber. Note the packed US Marine Corps and USAF flightlines in the background. *No 1(F) Squadron*

Below: Harriers flew missions against regime targets as well as flying Close Air Support (CAS) for troops on the ground. This machine carries a new Enhanced Paveway II LGB on its inner wing pylon. *No 1(F) Squadron*

Bottom: This Harrier GR7 sported a flamboyant sharksmouth as well as mission marks, reportedly to counter the similar markings applied to USAF A-10s operating in the same region! *No 1(F) Squadron*

Top: Harrier trio – three GR7s flown by No 1(F) Squadron pilots pose for the camera. Note that the furthest aircraft carries the Joint Reconnaissance Pod (JRP), which was loaned from the Jaguar force to give the Harriers a reconnaissance capability in the latter part of the conflict. *No 1(F) Squadron*

Above: RAF Harriers flew missions in the highest threat environments – here a GR7 cruises high above the Iraqi capital Baghdad. Pilots used ingenious methods to positively identify (PID) targets, including image-stabilised binoculars. *No 1(F) Squadron*

Below: During Operation 'Telic', coalition assets flew missions around the clock. The Harriers were in the thick of the action from the outset. *Crown Copyright*

Above: **A pair of Harrier GR7s punch out decoy flares, designed to spoof heat-seeking missile systems. These Harriers are in two different weapons configurations. The aircraft on the right carries Legacy Paveway II LGBs on outer pylons, while the aircraft on the left carries Enhanced Paveway IIs (EPW2s) on the inner wing pylons. The inner pylons were the only points on the GR7 configured for these new weapons.** *via No 1(F) Squadron*

Left: **A pair of GR7s stop off at a US Marine Corps FARP (Forward Arming and Refuelling Point) at An Numan in Iraq.** *No 1(F) Squadron*

Below: **The Al Jaber Harrier detachment of Nos 1(F) and IV(AC) Squadrons.** *No 1(F) Squadron*

Right: **The Tornado F3s in the Gulf were stationed at PSAB and flew pure air defence missions, though without engagement.** *Crown Copyright*

BATTLING BASRA

There were fascinating examples of ingenuity from all Coalition forces deployed for the conflict. In the battle around Basra for example, the RAF came up with a clever plan to reduce collateral damage and still tackle Iraqi armour that had been moved into residential areas. Instead of using high explosive bombs that would damage the civilian buildings around which the targets had taken refuge, the RAF reverted to using 1,000lb concrete-filled 'blue' practice bombs, fitted with Paveway laser guidance kits. As the Iraqi forces played the familiar card of placing military equipment near civilians, the concrete bombs were used to attack tanks and equipment even if parked in a narrow street with a high degree of success.

RULING THE SKIES

The RAF Tornado F3s operated air defence missions from PSAB in Saudi Arabia armed with the MBDA ASRAAM and Sky Flash missiles. A handful of F3s had been hastily modified to take on a Suppression of Enemy Air Defence (SEAD) role, for which they would have been equipped with the ALARM anti-radiation missile. However, the decision was taken not to deploy these aircraft, despite them being ready and highly capable. The F3s enjoyed total air superiority, and did not see any enemy action.

Below: **The RAF Tornado F3 force was on alert from the start, operating from Prince Sultan AB (PSAB), Saudi Arabia.** *Crown Copyright*

100

Top: **Although this image was taken at Basra after the war had finished, RAF Canberra PR9 reconnaissance aircraft deployed for 'Telic' to support the highly-classified western desert Scud-suppression missions. The black fairing under the rear fuselage of this aircraft is related to the type's classified datalink.** *Crown Copyright*

Centre: **The RAF's No 51 Squadron operates three potent Nimrod R1 electronic intelligence (ELINT) aircraft. These were in high demand from coalition planners during Operation 'Telic' and this one was seen at Cyprus on its way down south.** *Richard Flagg*

Above: **RAF Hercules (such as this C4) operated to a hectic schedule ferrying equipment and supplies into theatre.** *Crown Copyright*

STRONG SUPPORT

The Royal Air Force brought several key assets to the Coalition for Operation 'Iraqi Freedom'. The RAF's Canberra PR9 reconnaissance aircraft of No 39(1 PRU) Squadron are fitted with a camera and datalink system that enables them to fulfil similar role to the USAF's U-2S. They can to obtain high-quality imagery from long stand-off ranges, and downlink it (in near real-time) to any suitably equipped ground station. Compared to the U-2, the Canberra is understood to be less vulnerable to damage from high-altitude clear air turbulence frequently encountered in the Middle East's more mountainous regions. The two Canberras deployed to cover operations over the western Iraqi desert were reportedly airborne for up to eight hours each day using both EO-POROP and panoramic reconnaissance equipment to search for hostile activity.

The Nimrod R1 was another RAF platform in demand from Coalition air commanders. The R1 is broadly similar in equipment fit and role to the USAF's RC-135V/W Rivet Joint, fulfilling a SIGINT (Signals Intelligence) role. This entails gathering both ELINT (Electronic Intelligence – details and locations of enemy radar emitters) and COMINT (Communications Intelligence – intelligence derived from enemy communications traffic). Although the RAF Nimrod R1s have hitherto been associated with a passive listening role, there is no reason they should not be used in conjunction with missile-carrying Suppression of Enemy Air Defence (SEAD) aircraft as assistant targeting platforms for this role – in the same way that USAF RC-135s are used in conjunction with HARM-shooting F-16CJs.

Also providing reconnaissance imagery over Iraq were the six RAF Nimrod MR2s from No 206 Squadron that had deployed to Prince Sultan AB. They had been hurriedly fitted with new Wescam electro-optical turrets under the starboard wing. These aircraft provided additional 'eyes' over the battlefield for Coalition commanders using the type's onboard systems.

Top: **On final approach into Baghdad International Airport, an RAF C-130J punches out salvos of decoy flares for protection against hostile ground fire.** *USAF*

Above: **An RAF Puma HC1 pilot speeds across the desert at low-level ready to re-supply a forward position. A total of seven Pumas from No 33 Squadron at RAF Benson deployed to Kuwait for Operation 'Telic'.** *Crown Copyright*

Left: **You can almost hear the 'whump' of the rotor blades as this RAF Chinook HC2 comes in to land at a dusty desert strip. The 'brown out' conditions in the desert proved extremely hazardous for helicopter crews.** *Crown Copyright*

Top right: **RAF brothers – the workhorses of the battlefield. A Chinook HC2 of No 18 Squadron leads a Puma HC1 of No 33 Squadron. Both types were equipped with extensive defensive aids suites (DAS) for protection against hostile Iraqi groundfire.** *Crown Copyright*

Centre right: **An RAF Chinook HC2 of No 18 Squadron turns and burns as the loadmaster makes his external checks.** *No IX(B) Squadron*

The RAF's C-130 Hercules, C-17, VC10 and TriStar force worked around the clock to keep supplies, equipment and fuel flowing. The RAF also maintained a pair of VC10 C1Ks at RAF Akrotiri specifically to medevac personnel from theatre. This included both battlefield casualties and those injured in the ordinary course of events. Each aircraft was fitted with stretchers and personnel from No 4626 Squadron, Royal Auxiliary Air Force.

ROYAL NAVY

The Royal Navy carrier HMS *Ark Royal*, and some 3,000 Royal Marines, sailed for the Mediterranean on 11 January, with Defence Secretary Geoff Hoon stating that Saddam Hussein needed to be presented with 'a clear and credible threat of force'. The carrier abandoned its usual complement of Harriers to become a helicopter and supply platform to support the assault on Iraq from the Persian Gulf. HMS *Ocean* also sailed with 10 Sea King HC4s of 845NAS; and six Royal Marines Lynx AH7 and Gazelle AH1s of 847NAS were also embarked. The ships carried troops from 40 and 42 Commando, Royal Marines, and represented a potent show of strength. The Marines and the Westland Sea King HC4s were in the thick of the action from the first night as they assaulted the Al Fawr peninsula to take the docks at Umm Qasr. RAF Chinooks from No 18 Squadron also operated from the decks of the 'Ark' as they ferried equipment, troops and supplies to the battle. Sadly the carrier lost two of its Airborne Early Warning Sea King ASaC7s from 849NAS on 22 March in a tragic mid-air collision.

Top: **The Royal Navy sent HMS *Ark Royal* to the Persian Gulf, with 849NAS Sea King ASaC7s on board.** *Royal Navy*

Above: **A Royal Navy Sea King HC4 taxies at Basra Airport as British forces secured the airfield as a forward base.** *Jeremy Flack/API*

Left: **A Sea King HC4 of 845NAS lifts and a Chinook HC2 of No 18 Squadron prepares to start as supplies are ferried to British troops on the Al Faw peninsula from HMS *Ark Royal*.** *Crown Copyright*

BRITISH ARMY AIR CORPS

The Army Air Corps provided a further vital capability around the Basra region throughout the campaign with 10 Gazelle AH1s and 12 Lynx AH7s from 3 Regiment supporting British Army activity in the area. The AAC Lynx flew patrols over the oil refineries, pipelines and power lines in the areas surrounding Basra, to help prevent sabotage, in addition to conducting surveillance and reconnaissance flights. The Lynx operated as part of 16 Air Assault Brigade and fired over 100 Raytheon BGM-71 TOW anti-armour missiles – with 34 Army Air Corps and Royal Navy Lynx flying over 2,900hrs during the combat phase of Operation 'Telic'.

The Army's Lynx AH7s sent to the region had been upgraded with NVG-compatible cockpits, new defensive aids systems (DAS), sand filters, improved communications and new air traffic control systems.

Top right: **An Army Lynx equipped with door-mounted GPMG (General Purpose Machine Gun) on patrol near Basra.** *Crown Copyright*

Centre right: **Providing vital links on the battlefield, a 3 Regiment AAC Gazelle heads for its next task.** *Crown Copyright*

Below right: **A spotlight-equipped Gazelle AH1 lifts from its pad. The AAC deployed 10 of these utility helicopters.** *Crown Copyright*

Below: **An Army Air Corps (AAC) Lynx AH7 prepares to touch down on a makeshift heli-pad near Basra. The Army's 3 Regiment deployed 12 Lynx in support of Operation 'Telic'.** *Crown Copyright*

Unmanned action

Non-stop, real-time aerial reconnaissance was seen, from the outset, as a vital factor in the initial Coalition artillery assault. Larkhill-based 32 Regiment RA despatched an advance 'TAC Party' Group (from 18 Battery) to Kuwait City in January 2003. This advanced group was tasked with determining how and where best to deploy its Phoenix UAVs onto the battlefield. In the meantime some 39 Phoenix were shipped out through Marchwood Port. When the assault began, the Phoenix operation (which was in fact a composite unit, made up by 18 and 22 Battery) was deployed to the frontline in four Flight Troops, with each Troop being allocated with eight UAVs. During the first 36 hours of the campaign Phoenix UAVs provided continuous day and night cover, flying 18 missions over some of the most hostile territory around Basra. Shortly afterwards, Battery HQ was established inside Iraq at Shaibah airfield with reconnaissance flights centred upon Basra and the surrounding areas. Phoenix was used to assess the levels of enemy presence at the oil fields on the Al Faw peninsula, to provide targeting cues for US Predators and to monitor traffic movements on the road between Basra and Baghdad.

These potent little UAVs completed 138 operational sorties during the campaign and, given the extreme climate, battle losses were inevitable. Whilst the primary role for Phoenix was to locate targets, a number of the UAVs were launched on 'one-way' missions. These aircraft provided real–time reconnaissance until the fuel supply was exhausted. Some 23 Phoenix UAV flights ended in the UAV being damaged beyond repair, shot down, or missing in action. A further 13 sustained damage that was repairable.

Operation 'Falconer': Australia in Operation 'Iraqi Freedom'

Left: **Two Australian Army Aviation Corps CH-47Ds punch out self-protection flares from their bolt-on dispensers fitted just above the rear fuselage ramp whilst operating over Iraqi territory on 22 April 2003.** *ADF*

Below: **Carrying a single GBU-12 500lb LGB under each wing, a No 75 Squadron F/A-18A takes on fuel from a USAF KC-135 prior to heading into southern Iraq.** *ADF*

The Coalition opposed to Saddam Hussein's Ba'ath Party during Operation 'Iraqi Freedom' not only included the US and Britain, but the contribution made by a third coalition member was also vital to the war effort.

As in Operation 'Enduring Freedom' (OEF) in Afghanistan in late 2001, Australia committed both personnel and equipment to the fight in Iraq on a large scale.

On 1 February 2003, the Australian government announced that it would forward deploy both C-130 Hercules and F/A-18 Hornets and an Air Forward Command element to the Middle East Area of Operations (MEAO). The latter, according to an Australian Defence Force (ADF) spokesman, would be 'responsible for co-ordinating air operations with Coalition partners, and providing national control of Royal Australian Air Force (RAAF) assets'.

Recently expanded, thanks to substantial funding by the US government, Al Udeid was chosen as the primary operating location for the bulk of the RAAF aircraft allocated to the impending campaign. Al Udeid also accommodated the USAF's 379th Air Expeditionary Wing, as well as numerous RAF, US Navy and US Marine Corps assets.

The Australian deployment got underway as Operation 'Bastille' on 7 February 2003 when three C-130 Hercules (two tactically configured C-130Hs from No 36 Squadron and a strategically configured C-130J from No 37 Squadron) departed RAAF Richmond. These were followed on 9 February by 14 F/A-18A Hornets from No 75 Squadron from RAAF Tindal.

Finally, on 21 February, three Australian Army Aviation Corps CH-47D Chinooks from C Squadron, 5th Aviation Regiment were flown out to Kuwait aboard USAF C-5B Galaxys.

Having been quickly returned to flying status alongside US Army assets at Camp Doha, Kuwait, the Chinooks were allocated to an Australian Special Forces Task Group. Aside from the three CH-47Ds and personnel from 5th Aviation Regiment, the Task Group was comprised of a Special Air Service (SAS) squadron from the newly-established Incident Response Regiment and a quick reaction support force consisting of commandos from the 4th Battalion, Royal Australian Regiment (4RAR).

Already in-theatre were two RAAF P-3C Orions that had arrived in the Gulf in January 2003 at the start of a 12-month-long deployment as part of Operation 'Slipper', the ADF's ongoing commitment to the 'War on Terrorism'. Flying alongside American P-3Cs of VP-1 and EP-3E Aries IIs of VQ-1, the two Australian Orions from No 92 Wing (consisting of Nos 10 and 11 Squadrons) had flown surveillance flights in the Gulf of Oman in the weeks leading up to OIF.

The final aerial assets committed to Operation 'Falconer' were a trio of helicopters embarked on the Royal Australian Navy (RAN) vessels HMAS *Kanimbla*, HMAS *Anzac* and HMAS *Darwin*. Serving as flagship for the RAN frigates in-theatre, the amphibious warfare vessel *Kanimbla* was home to a solitary Sea King Mk50A of HS-817, while *Anzac* and *Darwin* each had a single S-70B-2 Seahawk of HS-816 embarked.

HORNET AT WAR

Australian fighter aircraft hadn't seen combat since July 1953 when No 77 Squadron Meteor F8s conducted their last ground attack missions of the Korean War. The last time the RAAF had dropped a bomb in anger was on 30 May 1971, when a No 2 Squadron Canberra B20 attacked a Viet Cong stronghold in South Vietnam. More recently, the RAAF sent four F/A-18s to Diego Garcia to provide terminal air cover for the base, which was home to USAF B-52Hs and B-1Bs committed to Operation 'Enduring Freedom'. The US government was again quick to approach the RAAF for OIF.

As the Coalition launched its first air strikes on 20 March, the RAAF Hornets of No 75 Squadron Hornets were airborne right from the start. Typically flying in pairs or as four-ships, the Hornet pilots initially flew defensive counter air (DCA) sorties for 'high value' force multiplier aircraft such as E-3 Sentry AWACS platforms, strategic reconnaissance aircraft (RC-135s and E-8 J-STARS) and aerial tankers.

The unit's CO, Wg Cdr 'Steve' gave an insight into these early missions soon after the conflict had commenced; 'The aircrews were basically given a vulnerability period — a period for which they were responsible to defend coalition forces, not just in the air. Our specific job was to defend US aircraft against threats from Iraqi jets, and we undertook the mission for the whole time they were allocated to our sector. In many ways, these early missions were really the next step up from the training that all the aircrews and the maintenance and supply people have been exercising for many years. The scale of the conflict here is enormous, however, and that is new to all of us. Having said that, we have nevertheless been able to come across the globe, plug into a major theatre of conflict and be very successful at our mission'.

DCA sorties over southern Iraq typically lasted between five and six hours, and saw the jets refuelling three or four times from Coalition tankers due to the considerable transit times from Al Udeid to the Iraqi area of operations. Flt Lt 'Peter' recalled; 'You'd pretty much cross over into Iraq with full tanks. Although most DCA sorties lasted around six hours, some of those I was involved in turned out to be nine-hour marathons. This meant that you were strapped into the jet for up to 10-and-a-half hours from the time you had started up until finally shutting down at mission end. It was like being strapped to a kitchen chair and put in a phone box for 10-and-a-half hours. On top of that, people were shooting at you!'

As the air war intensified, and the potential threat posed by the Iraqi AF failed to materialise, No 75 Squadron reverted almost exclusively to flying interdiction and close air support (CAS) missions for Coalition ground forces advancing into Iraq. Grp Capt William Henman, Officer Commanding the Hornets

in the MEAO, described to the Australian press exactly how his crews were tasked during the conflict; 'All mission planning, execution and debriefing was conducted in accordance with the existing doctrinal USAF Air Tasking Order (ATO) cycle that was generated from the Coalition Air Operations Centre (CAOC) on a daily basis. Australian aircraft were thus tasked just as any other coalition missions. The RAAF squadron and support elements were essentially 'embedded' into the USAF Air Expeditionary Wing organisation at the host third nation base'.

Left: **An RAAF Hornet pilot goes through pre-flight checks as he prepares for another mission over Iraq.** *ADF*

Below: **During OIF, RAAF Hornets occasionally worked with US Navy carrier-based aircraft. Here, a No 77 Squadron machine seconded to No 75 Squadron awaits its turn to tank over Kuwait. Behind it are two F/A-18Cs from VFA-27, embarked on the USS** *Kitty Hawk* **(CV-63). All three jets are carrying GBU-12s, although the Australian Hornet is the only one with a centreline tank and wingtip AIM-9Ls.** *ADF*

The effectiveness of the RAAF Hornets in-theatre was further enhanced by the secondment of current No 81 Wing pilots to the CAOC, where they were heavily involved in the development of the ATO and the joint target lists. Thanks to their strategic placement, these individuals were able to exert significant influence on how No 75 Squadron's modest assets were employed throughout the campaign.

When flying dedicated strike missions, RAAF Hornets were typically configured with two 2,000lb GBU-10 LGBs, a targeting pod, three tanks and Sidewinders for self-protection – later in the war, when the unit switched to the CAS role, the GBU-10s were replaced by lighter GBU-12 '500 pounders'. The first pre-planned Australian strike sorties were conducted on 23 March, the aircraft being part of a larger coalition strike package that

Top: **Two Hornets sit on the ramp at Al Udeid, ready for their next sortie towards the end of Operation 'Falconer'. Note the mission markings on the aircraft in the foreground.** *ADF*

Below: **The busy flightline at Al Udeid, with RAAF Hornets heading the line.** *RAF No 12(B) Squadron*

included USAF fighters and US Navy or US Marine Corps EA-6B Prowler electronic warfare aircraft.

Interdiction missions were flown primarily against targets in southern Iraq, RAAF Hornets bombing a variety of static military targets such as fuel dumps, bunkers and ammunition storage facilities. Elements of the Iraqi 10th Armoured Division were also attacked during late March, as was a regional intelligence and security headquarters in southern Iraq and the Republican Guard's Medina Division. Emphasising the multi air force make up of the strike packages, on 29 March two Hornets dropped four GBU-10s on a command headquarters as part of a coalition formation sortied from Al Udeid that included US Navy Tomcats (land-based F-14As from VF-154, put ashore from USS *Kitty Hawk* (CV-63) to act as dedicated target designators for Hornets and Tornado GR4s) and two RAF Tornados.

The first 14 days of the conflict saw RAAF Hornets regularly flying 12 sorties per day and by 3 April, the Australian jets had completed 130 combat sorties (including 70 strike missions) totalling roughly 700 hours. The sortie rate gradually dropped to between six and 10 flights a day from 5 April onwards as US

forces moved into Baghdad, leaving the Hornets with fewer targets to strike in the south of Iraq. By then, No 75 Squadron was almost exclusively flying CAS missions in support of ground forces such as the US Army's V Corps and the 1st Marine Expeditionary Force.

On 11 April the unit got to operate with Australian SAS and 4RAR Commandos when Hornets provided CAS for the capture of the Iraqi base at Al Asad, 180km west of Baghdad. Despite no bombs being dropped, it marked the first time that the RAAF had provided CAS for Australian ground forces since the Vietnam War. This was one of the last actions undertaken by the SAS in OIF, and it found 51 MiG-21s and MiG–25s, assorted helicopters, AAA batteries and a large store of ordnance and ammunition hidden within the base perimeter.

Following the fall of Baghdad on 9 April, the Hornets joined other Coalition assets by turning attentions on the Ba'athist stronghold of Tikrit. The RAAF Hornets bombed parked aircraft, tanks and troop positions around the southern outskirts of Tikrit during CAS missions flown in support of US Marines of Task Force Tripoli. All these targets were laser-designated and identified by Forward Air Controllers, these strikes being flown in advance of the Marines' attack on the city. Within minutes of the fast jets clearing the area, American main battle tanks drove into central Tikrit and seized the city following fierce street fighting.

Combat missions gradually tailed off after this, and No 75 Squadron dropped its last bombs on 17 April. The unit flew its final combat mission 10 days later, followed by its last training mission in-theatre on 2 May. All 14 aircraft returned to RAAF Tindal on 14 May, followed by the bulk of the 250 ground and support personnel the next day.

In its four months of active service in the MEAO, No 75 Squadron had flown 2,300hrs during the course of 670 sorties, including 1,800 hours on 350 combat missions. A total of 122 LGBs were dropped, and all munitions expended were precision guided.

Left: **Wearing the Southern Cross markings of No 3 Squadron on its tail, F/A-18A A21-14 taxies out at the start of the final Operation 'Falconer' mission to be flown by the RAAF, on 27 April 2003. Typically, the fighter carries a single GBU-12 under each wing.** *ADF*

Below: **With their desert camo flightsuits devoid of rank tabs, name tags or squadron emblems, four Australian Hornet pilots pose for the camera shortly after completing a sortie in early April 2003.** *ADF*

Above: **Australian SAS and 4RAR Commandos on patrol at Al Asad air base on 11 April 2003, having found a camouflaged MiG-25PU. This was just one of 51 fast jets found by Special Forces at this location 180km west of Baghdad.** *ADF*

QUIET ACHIEVERS

Little was reported of the role played by the two RAAF P-3s deployed for Operation 'Falconer'. Chief of the Air Force Air Marshal Angus Houston was quoted as saying; 'The P-3s are very much the quiet achievers. They have been flying every night, operating with the carrier battle groups. They were essentially guarding them against asymmetric type threats — small fast boats approaching the carrier. So they were out there using their sensors to enhance the protection of the carrier battle groups'.

Flying alongside US Navy P-3Cs, the Australian Orions kept a close watch on the strategically important Khawr Abd Allah waterway, which led to Iraq's sole port at Umm Qasr. The Orion's FLIR and various other electro-optical (EO) and ESM sensors proved critical when scouring the waterway at night, or in bad weather.

There is also a possibility that one of the deployed aircraft was one of the RAAF's highly-classified EP-3Cs fitted with E-Systems intelligence-gathering ELINT equipment.

HERCULEAN HELP

Although accounting for barely 3% of the 96 Coalition C-130s committed to OIF, the trio of deployed RAAF Hercules at one point carried an amazing 15% of the tonnage hauled in the MEAO by the ubiquitous Lockheed transporter. Air Marshal Houston explained how this was achieved; 'Our C-130J drew a lot of attention when it arrived in Gulf, and together with the two H-models, the aircraft carried a lot more freight than the American examples in-theatre. We achieved this by carrying less fuel, we operate to tighter fuel reserves and we operate to the performance charts that come from the manufacturer. As a consequence, we lifted most of the heavy C-130 cargo'.

The two C-130Hs (each fitted with an electronic warfare self-protection suite) flew tactical missions into forward operating bases throughout the region, including inserting Commandos

Below: **Two C-130Hs of No 36 Squadron are seen disembarking ADF personnel soon after arriving in the MEAO in mid-February 2003. These machines were used in the tactical role throughout Operation 'Falconer', and later became some of the first transport aircraft to fly into the newly captured Baghdad Airport on 13 April.** *ADF*

Right: The crew of a No 36 Squadron C-130H prepare for take-off from a hazy Baghdad International Airport during Operation 'Baghdad Assist'. The H-model Hercules operated by the RAAF in-theatre were all fitted with electronic warning systems, allowing them to manually deploy chaff and IR decoy flares. Operating both day and night (with NVGs), crews would typically fly a low-level 500ft tactical approach into Baghdad. Once on the ground, US Army security personnel secured the immediate area surrounding the C-130, which kept its engines running. US Army forklift trucks and ground personnel would then unload the Hercules for a rapid departure in around 15mins. Despite the airport being secured in mid-April, shoulder-mounted ground-to-air missiles remained a serious threat. *ADF*

Below: A solitary No 37 Squadron C-130J was assigned to Operation 'Falconer'. The aircraft was configured for long-haul strategic flights, as the type has yet to be operationally cleared for tactical missions with the RAAF. The three deployed RAAF C-130s accounted for only 3% of the Coalition's 'Herks' operating in OIF, but, through clever operating procedures, the trio became greatly admired for the high workload and at one point carried an amazing 15% of the MEAO hauled tonnage. *ADF*

Seahawks and a Sea King Mk50A, also made a valued contribution to the war. This was the second Gulf War for the S-70B-2s of HS-816 as the unit had made its combat debut with the helicopter during Operation 'Damask' (during 'Desert Storm') in 1991. In 2003, single helicopters embarked HMAS *Anzac* ('Akubra' flight) and HMAS *Darwin* ('Agro' flight). The Seahawks' role in Operations 'Slipper' (the vessels had been in the Arabian Gulf conducting Maritime Interception Operations with US and British ships since early February 2003) and 'Falconer' was very similar to the part played by the

and their Land Rovers into Iraq on 13 April 2003. That same day, the first RAAF Hercules was sent into Baghdad Airport carrying medical supplies as part of Operation 'Baghdad Assist'. The solitary C-130J was configured for long-haul strategic flights (the type has yet to be operationally cleared for tactical missions with the RAAF), and it was supplanted by two more J-models on 13 April as part of 'Baghdad Assist'. The latter flew some 20,000kg of medical supplies into the MEAO from RAAF Richmond, with the cargo then being offloaded and transferred to the C-130Hs for onward delivery to Baghdad. By early May 2003, the Australian C-130s had flown more than 130 missions, carrying over 1,360 tonnes of cargo and 1,500 troops.

helicopter in the first conflict. HS-816's primary mission was to help patrol the Khor Abd Allah (KAA) waterway between Iraq and Kuwait, which led to the strategic port of Umm Qasr. Surface co-ordination with the myriad of Coalition vessels in the area, as well as airspace deconfliction proved to be two of the more challenging tasks facing the helicopter crews on a daily basis.

With literally hundreds of rotary and fixed-wing aircraft operating in an area of just 30nm surrounding the Al Faw peninsula, the risk of aerial collisions was a real one, as was tragically illustrated by the accident which befell the two 849NAS Sea King ASaC7 on 22 March.

On Day Three of the campaign, 'Agro' flight's S-70 became the first Australian helicopter to support the mine countermeasures effort in the KAA, operating in conjunction with a US Navy SH-60 supporting two MH-53E Sea Dragons towing anti-mine sleds.

'AGRO' AND 'AKUBRA'

Although the RAAF provided the bulk of the aircraft deployed to the MEAO for Operation 'Falconer', a modest Royal Australian Navy helicopter force, consisting of two S-70

Following the capture of Umm Qasr, and the eradication of enemy forces in the Al Faw peninsula, *Darwin's* Seahawk crew turned its attention to shuttling humanitarian aid from HMAS *Kanimbla* to Kuwait.

Anzac's 'Akubra' flight spent much of its time conducting surface search patrols of the KAA waterway, where crews developed their 'dhow herding' techniques. Iraqi dhows would start their run for the Persian Gulf around sunset, and the Seahawk, operating in the 'sheepdog' role, would have them all turned around and heading back north by midnight. Aside from intercepting dhows, the 'Akubra' crew also encountered the 'Marine Mammal Mk7' in-theatre; the US Navy's mine-seeking dolphins. Indeed, the flight was often asked to look out for them due to their propensity to go on unauthorised 'swimabouts'!

The bare statistics for the Seahawk flights reveal just how busy both helicopters were, *Darwin's* S-70 flying 275.8 hours during the course of 62 'Slipper' and 27 'Falconer' sorties. *Anzac's* flight flew a total of 302.5 hours and 125 sorties.

'SHARK 07'

The RAN's heavy-hauler in Operation 'Falconer' was Sea King Mk50A N16-118/907, 'Shark 07' of HS-817, which was embarked on the *Kanimbla* and despatched to the Persian Gulf from Sydney on 24 January 2003. The flight found itself busy from the moment it arrived in-theatre, and in March the solitary Sea King set a squadron record by flying 126.5hrs (out of a total of 205.9 hours for the entire deployment). This was more than the combined monthly total for all the remaining HS-817 helicopters during the same period.

The helicopter performed logistics support (carrying 422 passengers and 226,350lb of freight), medical evacuations, surface search co-ordination and combat support and

Below: HS-817's Sea King Mk50A (N16-118) is un-tethered on the flightdeck of HMAS *Kanimbla* on 28 February 2003. This helicopter was flown hard during Operation 'Falconer', with the US Navy's HC-2 Det2 crews commenting that the 'Aussies seemed to get everywhere' during the vessel's long spell in the Arabian Gulf. *ADF*

Above: HS-817's Sea King Mk50A overflies the Iraqi barge *Naihawa* and the tug *Jumhuriyah* on 22 March 2003. A boarding party despatched from HMAS *Kanimbla* captured these vessels after it was suspected that they might be carrying illegal cargo. A search soon discovered some 86 Lug and Manta mines, as well as a cache of small arms and semi-automatic weapons. The mines were discovered in the barge hold, which is designed to store oil, while the small arms and automatic weapons were found in the bilge, under mattresses and on the bridge. *ADF*

reconnaissance for the RAN's Clearance Diving Team 3 (CDT3). The latter was helping US Naval Special Clearance Team One and the Royal Navy's Fleet Diving Unit Two clear mines from the port of Umm Qasr.

On 25 March, 'Shark 07' became the first RAN helicopter to land in Iraq when it dropped off personnel at Khaw Az Zubayr. The helicopter made an unscheduled return to this location on 13 April following a single engine failure over Iraq's Al Faw peninsula during a low-level reconnaissance flight. *Kanimbla* flight commander, Lt Cdr Paul Moggach, was at the controls, and he takes up the story; 'The flight profile involved a number of low-level passes within one nautical mile of the northern shore of the Al Faw peninsula. These were being conducted at speeds of 50-70kt and altitudes of between 100-200ft. The helicopter was transitioned into a low (40ft), slow (20kt ground speed) pass along any suspected ordnance locations so that embarked divers could assess the site. We were about 1.5hrs into the sortie, and had made significant progress down the peninsula when I saw a large pile of mortar rounds lying on the ground near our flightpath. I rolled the Sea King into a 30-degree angle of bank turn to the left and started to descend, aiming to position the helicopter so that the divers could identify what type of mortar rounds we had discovered.

'The helicopter was about 210 degrees through the 360-degree turn when things started to go pear-shaped. At a height of about 40ft, and at 30kt airspeed, I heard an annoying whining sound above my head. In the time that it took to think 'What the hell is that?', the number one engine shut itself

down, leaving us in a rather unenviable position. We didn't know it at the time. But the number one engine input coupling, which connects the free power turbine to the gearbox, had internally fractured, meaning that the engine was now free to drive itself to destruction. Fortunately, the Sea King engines have a self-protection system that will automatically shut the engine down in just this circumstance.

'A running landing is normally the option that would be taken in these circumstances. However, it all depends on the nature of the surface you intend landing on, in this case the surface was a soft, sandy, muddy texture covered with berms and levees, making the required running landing impossible. I was too low to effectively slow the aircraft into a zero-zero landing. The other thing that I vividly remember was that our likely landing point would have been in the exact location of the mortar rounds. The landing would certainly have been spectacular. That left me with only one option... fly away'.

And fly away Lt Cdr Moggach did, once he had got 100% power out of the remaining engine and crept up to 65kt at a height of just 20ft.

'We secured the faulty engine and made a decision to land at Az Zubayr, just 18nm up the river. Our ship was over 30nm away, and as tempting as it was to head home to mother, it just wasn't a viable option for a single engine landing. We knew that there was a Royal Navy forward operating base at Az Zubayr, and that they had a Sea King unit in residence. There was also a large concrete area suitable for the requisite running landing. We went through the checks and eventually conducted a safe landing'.

ABOVE AND BEYOND

The ADF's commitment to OIF in terms of the sheer number of aircraft it sent to the MEAO looks less than impressive when stacked up against the US or British contribution. However, the quality of the crews flying these machines, and the results they achieved, saw all three services 'punching above their weight capability', as Air Marshal Houston was pleased to point out in his post-war address.

Saddam's War Machine

THE THREAT OF THE IRAQI FORCES

During the 1991 Gulf War, Operation 'Desert Storm' severely degraded President Saddam Hussein's military might. However, as a result of having such a large force in the first place, Iraq managed to retain some of its potency and also sought to covertly re-develop its capabilities.

In the mid-1970s, Saddam Hussein launched a major arming effort in a bid to establish Iraq as a world superpower. The country invested heavily in combat aircraft, capability upgrades and weapons, T-72 main battle tanks, artillery systems, rocket development and small arms production. In the 1980s, Iraq began developing ballistic missiles, although these programmes were largely destroyed during Gulf War I, with a large number of Saddam's combat aircraft fleeing, and never returning.

However, the 1990s saw Iraq return to modest military growth in a bid to rebuild its conventional weapons stockpiles. Since 'Desert Storm', the United Nations had fought an uphill battle against Iraqi concealment and the requirement for Saddam to destroy his Weapons of Mass Destruction (WMD) and its capacity to develop and produce such weapons.

Sanctions imposed after Gulf War I not only affected Iraq's weapons production, but also its people. A fraction of the workforce that was involved in pre-Gulf War weapons programmes were still employed in the business. Iraqi weapon manufacturing was controlled by the Military Industrialisation Organisation (MIO), with this organisation believed to have run programmes at hundreds of sites around the country, ranging from small arms and ammunition production to the covert development and alleged production of WMD. As well as its well-documented chemical and biological weapons, nuclear weapons had also been studied (and possibly developed) under MIO programmes.

Of particular note was Saddam's integrated air and missile defence system, including a surveillance radar system to defeat cruise missile attacks. Indeed, the US was concerned over reports that Iraq planned to buy electronic warfare radar systems from Eastern Europe that would have the capability of detecting Stealth aircraft.

Iraq also sought to improve the capabilities of its S-75 Dvina (SA-2 'Guideline') SAMs. Under the terms of the UN ceasefire

Far left: **The Iraqi AF received around 50 MiG-29 'Fulcrums', with only a handful remaining in service at the start of Operation 'Iraqi Freedom'. None of these potent fighters even tried to get airborne once hostilities commenced.**

Below: **Not many Iraqi AF assets remained intact at the start of Operation 'Iraqi Freedom', and even fewer at the end. This battered MiG-21 stands guard at Shaibah AB.** *Jeremy Flack/API*

Above: **Australian Special Forces found a number of hidden Iraqi AF aircraft at Al Asad AB. This two-seat MiG-25PU was concealed under netting.** *ADF*

Inset: **The Iraqi AF had reportedly converted some of its aircraft into platforms to deliver deadly chemical weapons. This Aero L-29 Delfin was one of the suspects.**

agreement, Iraq was permitted to maintain a 150km missile programme, however, this and other programmes were feared to have exceeded these parameters.

Other pre-war reports from inside Iraq indicated that the trend of converting existing systems to fulfil new roles had continued. In 1997 it was reported that a Polish-made BZM18 crop duster had been modified to operate as an Unmanned Aerial Vehicle (UAV) capable of spraying chemical weapons and biological agents. It was also understood that the Iraqi administration had imported prohibited materials from abroad.

During Operation 'Desert Fox' in 1998, coalition aircraft struck Iraqi arms production facilities, however, the Iraqi military production machine remained resilient and by June 2000 it was well on the way to developing the short-range al Samoud ballistic missile. This missile fell within the 150km limitation, but the follow-on al Samoud II drew concern from weapons inspectors upon their re-entry to Iraq in late 2002. Indeed, investigation showed that this new missile exceeded the range limitation and was therefore ordered for destruction by the UN Inspectors.

AL QUWWAT AL JAWWIYA AL IRAQIYA: THE IRAQI AF

The Iraqi AF traces its roots back to the air arm that was established under British control in 1931. It was initially equipped with mainly British types, but, during the late 1960s, it began receiving new aircraft from the Soviet Union. Iraq also started to receive new aircraft from other western countries in the early 1970s, such as its French-supplied Mirage F1s.

During the first Gulf War, a large number of Iraqi AF pilots defected to Iran, giving the IRIAF a welcome boost in its assets as the aircraft were not returned at the end of hostilities. These included Mirage F1BQ/EQs, Su-24MK 'Fencer-Ds', MiG-29 'Fulcrums', Su-20 'Fitters', Su-22M 'Fitters', Su-25 'Frogfoots', MiG-23 'Floggers' and Il-78 'Midas' tankers.

At the end of 2002, the Iraqi air defence force was evaluated as having varying numbers of Mirage F1EQs, MiG-21s, MiG-23s, MiG-25s and MiG-29s, while its attack fleet included Mirage F1EQs, Su-20s, Su-22s, Su-24s and Su-25s. The transport and aerial tanker assets mainly consisted of An-24s, An-26s and Il-76/78s. All were known to have poor levels of serviceability. Indeed, an overall assessment put the

FRONT

Surface to Surface Missiles have been targeted for destruction.

BACK

FOR YOUR SAFETY

Abandon your weapons systems. Whether manned or unmanned, these weapons systems will be destroyed.

Left: **The many leaflets dropped by Coalition aircraft left Iraqi military personnel in no doubt as to what their actions should be.** *US DoD*

Iraqi AF fleet at around 300 combat aircraft, although only 50 fighters and 30 ground-attack aircraft were understood to remain operational (including 30 MiG-21PF/MF, 30 MiG-23ML, five MiG-25PDs and just four MiG-29s).

As Operation 'Iraqi Freedom' got underway it came as no surprise that the Iraqi AF put up no retaliation. The overall operational capability of Iraqi aviation was low, while the surface-to-air threat was assessed as 'medium to high'. The main threat to coalition aircraft consisted of the Iraqi Air Defence System incorporating early warning radars, visual observers and SAMs. Of primary concerns were the concentrated strategic SAMs around Baghdad's Super Missile Engagement Zone (Super MEZ) and the large number of tactical SAMs, Man Portable Air Defence Systems (MANPADS) and AAA being held in unknown locations.

Where was the Iraqi AF?

It seems that the regime had decided to disperse its fighters around the country prior to the outbreak of hostilities. Early reports of MiG-23s in cemeteries and on the perimeters of airfields emerged as the conflict began, with US commanders confidently stating 'If they fly, they die'. This time, the Iraqi AF knew better than to head for Iran, so what was airworthy remained firmly on the ground, or even underneath it…

Some suggest that certain broad-minded Iraqi AF commanders had struck a deal with Washington over the future of the Iraqi AF. The no-show may have been as result of this, coupled with the huge odds stacked against the Iraqi pilots and their ill-equipped aircraft. At the Iraqi AF's largest base at Al Taqqadum for example, the infrastructure of the base was left intact, but the dispersed fighters on the airfield were hit (though many of these were already derelict). It was later to be discovered that a number of previously airworthy aircraft had been disassembled and concealed, and even buried in the sand at the base.

Coalition Special Forces teams unearthed some 30 MiG and Sukhoi combat aircraft that had been crudely covered in plastic sheeting and subsequently buried (including an Electronic Intelligence (ELINT)-configured MiG-25RBT). These aircraft had little protection from the sand and are unlikely to ever fly again after this somewhat bizarre act. At Al Asad, around 51 intact MiGs were recovered, most of which had been placed under netting and in trees. Elsewhere decoys were found parked on Iraqi airfields — and even wooden mock-ups of long-retired Hawker Hunters were discovered.

Above: **The sands of Al Taqqadum AB concealed a number of Iraqi AF combat aircraft. As US forces moved in these were unearthed, with this MiG-25RBT being a particularly notable 'find'.** *USAF*

Below left: **At Tallil AB, this Iranian AF F-4 Phantom lies derelict with its engines still fitted. A tatty old Iraqi army boot illustrates yet another piece of abandoned military equipment.** *USAF*

Below right: **Iraqi air bases are littered with derelict airframes. This tail belongs to an Su-25 'Frogfoot'.** *USAF*

Clockwise, from top left: **An Iraqi AF MiG-23 'Flogger' that paid the ultimate price.**

A true classic – various ex-Iraqi AF Hawker Sea Furys were found abandoned at Shaibah, with this T20 being in particularly good condition considering its age. *Jeremy Flack/API*

Another wreck at Tallil is this Mi-4, once a workhorse of the Iraqi rotary fleet. *USAF*

The remains of a Zlin Z326 trainer, dumped at Shaibah AB. Much of the structure has been battered and twisted in the ravages of the desert. *Jeremy Flack/API*

A US soldier records this derelict MiG-29.

The daily US Central Command (CENTCOM) press briefing on 1 April gave an interesting insight into an AC-130 attack on the remote Iraqi H3 desert airfield. Video footage was described as the Herk gunship engaged 'Iraqi AF jets on the runway'. However, it was clear that the aircraft being destroyed were decoy Hunters, a MiG-17 and an Su-17. CENTCOM said; 'Obviously, we thought they were targets to take out and we continue to take out targets that can erode the regime'.

THE FUTURE

Lt Gen Muzahim Sa'b Hassan al-Tikriti, the commander of the Iraqi Air Defence command fell into US hands at the end of April 2003, with Iraqi AF Commander Hamid Raja Shalah al-Tikriti following on 14 June 2003. The fate of the many other Iraqi AF leaders was not made public, although officials that co-operated were believed to have been whisked away as the war unfolded.

Despite an announcement in mid-2003 that the old 400,000-strong Iraqi armed forces would be disbanded and replaced by a new Iraqi Civil Defence Corps (ICDC) of 35,000, it is believed that a modest air force will now be rejuvenated. Al Asad airfield 180km west of Baghdad was not heavily bombed by the Coalition and many believe that this airfield will form the basis for a new military air force infrastructure.

The high profile capture of Saddam in late 2003 (see 'After the Storm' chapter) further helped the Coaltion towards establishing stability in Iraq. Tensions continued to run high well into 2004. Coalition and Iraqi civilian casualties continued in the post-war environment, with Saddam loyalists and suicide bombers making almost daily news. The long-standing threat to Coalition aircraft had also not dissipated, with the pilots facing a threat as real as it was during the height of the air war. Hostile forces continued to operate and employ SA-7, SA-16 and SA-18 to target transport aircraft and battlefield helicopters operating in the region. The Iraqi military has ceased to exist, but in the post-Saddam era it remains clear that the terrorist tactics continue to have a deep impact on the rebuilding efforts for the Iraq of tomorrow.

Above: **Curiously, this Mi-6 at Shaibah had been sliced clean in half. It was just one of the many relics at this desert base.** *Jeremy Flack/API*

Above left: **The Iraqi AF may have retained a handful of Su-22 'Fitters'.**

Left: **An abandoned Iraqi SAM battery near Baghdad is inspected by US troops.** *USAF*

Below: **Al Asad AB, 180km west of Baghdad, could be used as the base for a future military air arm in Iraq.** *No 1(F) Squadron*

New Technology

Operation 'Iraqi Freedom' brought unprecedented levels of technology to the battlefield. A number of 'combat firsts' made the headlines, with both US and British forces rushing new capabilities into service to ensure the highest levels of weapon accuracy, time-critical information gathering and ultimately a swift and decisive outcome. Above all, the Coalition forces worked hard to minimise collateral damage and to do so they employed the latest precision weapons.

US TECHNOLOGY

Joint Direct Attack Munition (JDAM)

The JDAM made its combat debut during Operation 'Allied Force' in 1999 when B-2As delivered more than 600 of these lethally precise weapons. Guided by satellite using an onboard global positioning system (GPS)-aided inertial navigation system (INS), the weapon comes in various sizes and capabilities. Although it is also available in 500lb and 1,000lb (227kg and 454kg) varieties, the JDAMs dropped by the USAF bomber force mainly comprised the 2,000lb (907kg) GBU-31(V)1/B and GBU-31(V)3/B weapons. OIF marked the first time the GBU-31 was used by the F-14D Tomcat.

Below: **Red shirted US Navy ordnancemen load a Joint Direct Attack Munition (JDAM) on a VFA-37 F/A-18C Hornet.** *US Navy*

This US Navy Boeing F/A-18F Super Hornet pilot wears the new Joint Helmet Mounted Cueing System (JHMCS). The system allows the pilot to look at a target to cue weapons or sensors. *US Navy*

The AGM-154 Joint Stand-Off Weapon is an extremely accurate stand-off munition, but was only used in small numbers. This JSOW-toting F/A-18C of VFA-94 'Mighty Shrikes' bucks on the wire as it traps aboard USS *Nimitz* (CVN-68). *US Navy*

Above **A B-52H departs RAF Fairford with an impressive load of CBU-105 WCMD.** *Peter J. Cooper/Falcon Aviation*

CBU-105 WCMD

Referred to as a 'smart-guided' cluster bomb, the CBU-105 Wind Corrected Munitions Dispenser (WCMD) has built-in technology designed to correct the weapon's trajectory and therefore withstand any variable winds and atmospheric conditions encountered during its 'flight'. This serves to accurately navigate the weapon to its intended aim point at a predetermined altitude above an armoured formation. Upon reaching that altitude it disperses 10 BLU-108/B series parachute-stabilised sub-munitions equipped with infrared sensors that are programmed to detect the unique heat signatures of armoured vehicles. The sub-munitions then engage individual armoured vehicles by firing high-velocity shaped charges downward to penetrate the armour and destroy the vehicle with devastating effect.

Massive Ordnance Air Burst (MOAB)

Although reports of its use over Iraq remained unconfirmed, on 11 March 2003 the USAF conducted the first live test-drop of the massive precision-guided 21,500lb (9,752kg) conventional bomb. The Massive Ordnance Air Burst (MOAB) weapon, which is the most powerful non-nuclear weapon in existence, replaces the 15,000lb (6,800kg) BLU-82 'Commando Vault' (see right). Like the BLU-82, MOAB is intended to be air dropped from the cargo deck of a MC-130 Hercules. It differs from the earlier weapon however in being precision guided. While the earlier weapon relied on precise navigation to hit its target, the MOAB is guided by satellite via global positioning system (GPS) data. The precision guidance allows the delivery aircraft to operate at a much safer altitude than was required of the parachute-stabilised BLU-82.

USAF

Northrop Grumman AN/AAQ-28(V) Litening II

Some A-10A Thunderbolt IIs received the capability to carry the Litening II targeting pod in the run up to OIF. This 104th FS, 175th Wing Maryland ANG example carries the pod as it transits to the Persian Gulf. The pod was widely employed across a number of US assets during the conflict. *USAF*

BLU-82/B 'Commando Vault'

Designed to clear landing zones for helicopters, the BLU-82/B 'Daisy Cutter' was developed during the Vietnam War. Too large to be carried by conventional bombers the 15,000lb (6,804kg) weapons are deployed at high altitude from the cargo bay of C-130 transports. Basically a large tank constructed from .25in (6.35mm) steel, the BLU-82 is filled with a 12,600lb (5,715kg) explosive mixture. Mounted on an aerial delivery platform and cradle, a cargo extraction parachute pulls the store from the aircraft. Once airborne the weapon separates from the pallet and a stabilisation parachute is deployed. A 38in (965mm) fuse extension or a radar altimeter trigger mechanism causes the 'Big Blu' to detonate while still above the ground causing an explosion designed to level vegetation in an area approximately 260ft (79m) across without creating a large crater. The weapon's accuracy is dependent on the aircraft position and the timing of its release.

Prior to operations in Afghanistan, the BLU-82 was last used during Operation 'Desert Storm', when MC-130Es from the 8th Special Operations Squadron (SOS) dropped 11 of them on Iraqi forces. The first use of these bombs in support of Operation 'Iraqi Freedom' is believed to have taken place on 5 March 2003 when at least two examples were dropped over Republican Guard positions. (See below.)

BRITISH TECHNOLOGY
Storm Shadow

The MBDA Storm Shadow is a conventionally armed, long-range, all-weather, stand-off precision air-to-ground cruise missile designed to attack high-value targets. The weapon is typically used against well-defended targets and can be fitted with a 'broach' warhead to penetrate bunkers. It was pressed into service in early 2003 for the RAF Tornado GR4 following a trials programme led by the 'Dambusters' of No 617 Squadron at RAF Lossiemouth. Storm Shadow has a 'fire and forget' mode and is pre-programmed before the mission. The missile is fired at a long stand-off range from the target and navigates with digital terrain profile matching and GPS precision. As the weapon approaches the target, an automatic target recognition system compares the actual scene with a memorised programme of what it is looking for, therefore positively identifying the target to deliver a devastating blow whilst minimising collateral damage.

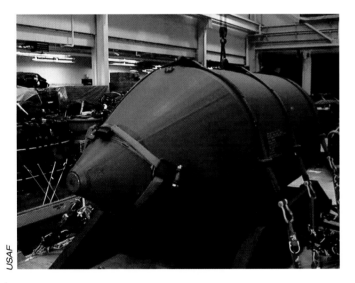

USAF

Above: On the first night of the war, RAF groundcrews prepare the first Storm Shadow missiles for No 617 Squadron Tornados at Ali al Salem AB, Kuwait. *Crown Copyright*

Left: Seen during the run up to OIF, a No 617 Squadron Tornado GR4 clutches a pair of Storm Shadows during clearance trials. *No 617 Squadron*

RAPTOR

The Reconnaissance Airborne Pod for Tornado (RAPTOR) is an Electro-Optical and Infra-Red 'recce' pod for the RAF Tornado GR4/4A. This stand-off system allows the Tornado to gather imagery of pre-planned or 'opportunity' targets, which can then be data-linked back to a ground station. RAPTOR is able to cover as many as 200 separate 'targets' in a single mission. The RAF currently has eight RAPTOR pods and the system was brought into service by No II(AC) Squadron at RAF Marham.

Below: **The RAPTOR reconnaissance pod is seen under the fuselage of this Tornado GR4 about to taxi out for a mission from Ali al Salem, Kuwait.** *No IX(B) Squadron*

Advanced Short-Range Air-to-Air Missile (ASRAAM)

The RAF's latest high-speed, high-agility heat-seeking air-to-air missile was carried by Tornado F3s for the first time in combat.

Air Launched Anti-Radiation Missile (ALARM)

The Air Launched Anti-Radiation Missile (ALARM) is designed to destroy or suppress enemy ground-based air defence systems. The weapon was used in the first Gulf War but in OIF the advanced new ALARM II was employed predominantly by the SEAD-specialist No IX(B) Squadron. ALARM operates by homing onto radar energy emitted from the target system. If the target is actively 'radiating', the missile can be launched straight at it to deliver a lethal attack. However, the missile can also be launched with pre-programmed target requirements in an area of known activity and will loiter on a parachute and wait for a radar to 'come on-line' before attacking.

ENHANCED PAVEWAY (EPW)

The Raytheon Enhanced Paveway II/III (EPW2/3) is an all-weather, day/night, Laser-Guided Bomb, modified to accommodate a Global Positioning System Aided Inertial Navigation System (GAINS). The weapon was carried by the RAF Tornado GR4s and Harrier GR7s and proved extremely effective in OIF.

Below: **An RAF Tornado GR4 carrying Enhanced Paveway IIs hooks up with a tanker before pressing towards its target.** *No 617 Squadron*

War Paint

In true wartime style, many units participating in Operation 'Iraqi Freedom' adorned aircraft with stunning noseart. The quality varied between squadrons and fleets and of particular note was the 'Political Correctness' of the artwork, with cartoon characters preferred over the more traditional female-orientated designs.

This chapter serves as an overview of the noseart highlights, providing complete rundowns of the USAF F-15E and RAF fleets deployed as well as samples from other types involved.

UNITED STATES AIR FORCE

F-15E Strike Eagle, 4th Fighter Wing

'DRAGON BETTY II'

'Shangri-La II'

'BACK FOR MORE – MAD DUCK IV'

'DARKNESS FALLS'

'THE BIRD OF PREY'

'SOUTHERN COMFORT – BAMA'

'MIGHTY MOUSE'

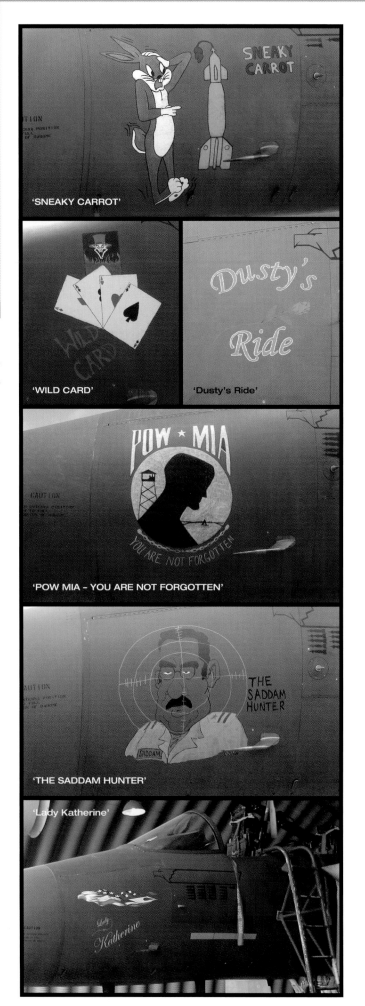

'SNEAKY CARROT'

'WILD CARD'

'Dusty's Ride'

'POW MIA – YOU ARE NOT FORGOTTEN'

'THE SADDAM HUNTER'

'Lady Katherine'

'4 WARNED'

'CAPTAIN AMERICA'

'A CRY FOR THE FALLEN'

'Memphis Belle III'

'Lucky'

'THE PUNISHER'

'CREEPING DEATH'

'493 NUMBER OF THE BEAST'

'SOUTHERN OUTLAW'

'WHAT GOES AROUND COMES AROUND'

'Dirty Bird'

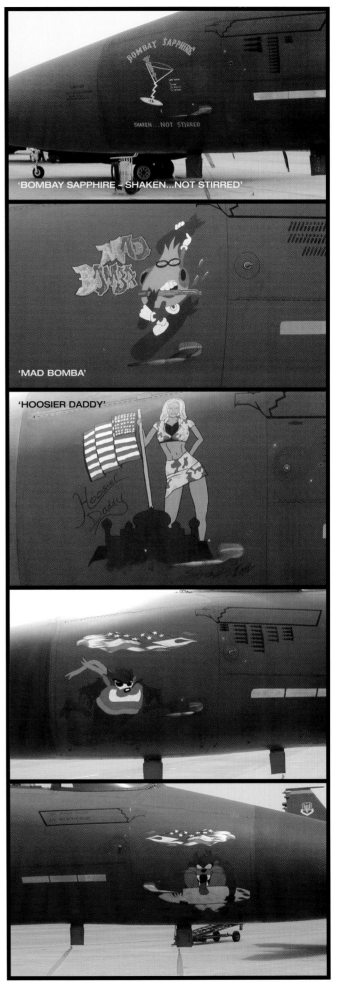

'BOMBAY SAPPHIRE – SHAKEN...NOT STIRRED'

'MAD BOMBA'

'HOOSIER DADDY'

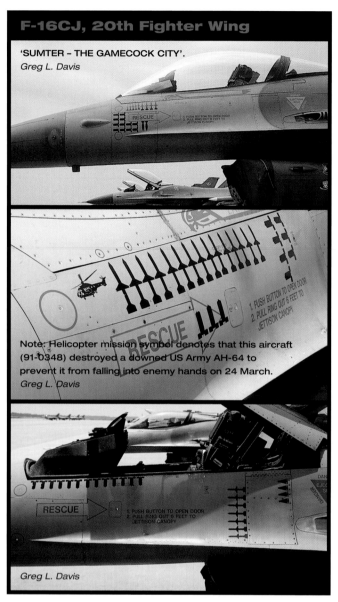

F-16CJ, 20th Fighter Wing

'SUMTER – THE GAMECOCK CITY'.
Greg L. Davis

Note: Helicopter mission symbol denotes that this aircraft (91-0348) destroyed a downed US Army AH-64 to prevent it from falling into enemy hands on 24 March.
Greg L. Davis

1. PUSH BUTTON TO OPEN DOOR
2. PULL RING OUT 6 FEET TO JETTISON CANOPY

RESCUE

Greg L. Davis

F-16CJ, 169th Fighter Wing, South Carolina ANG

RESCUE

Greg L. Davis

'SCOOTER'S SHOOTER'

'HOLTZ HUSTLER'

'COURTESY OF THE RED WHITE & BLUE'

RESCUE

Greg L. Davis

F-117A, 49th Fighter Wing

88-0842/HO, 8th FS. *USAF*

A/OA-10A, 118th FS, Connecticut ANG

'OH !!! THANK HEAVEN FOR 707!'. *Nate Leong*

'OH !!! THANK HEAVEN FOR 707!'. *Nate Leong*

OH !!! THANK HEAVEN FOR 707 !

'LET'S ROLL'. *Nate Leong*

B-52H, Barksdale & Minot AFBs

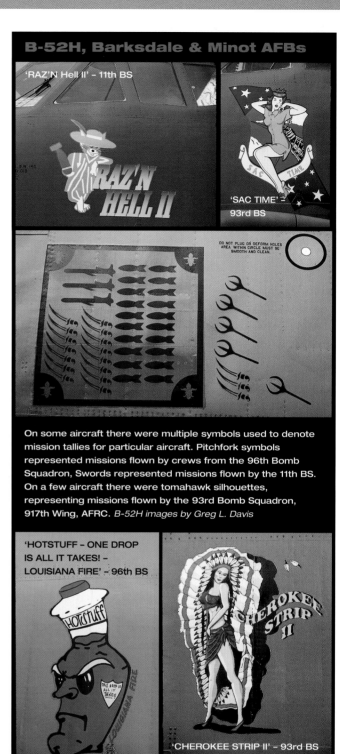

'RAZ'N Hell II' – 11th BS

'SAC TIME' – 93rd BS

On some aircraft there were multiple symbols used to denote mission tallies for particular aircraft. Pitchfork symbols represented missions flown by crews from the 96th Bomb Squadron, Swords represented missions flown by the 11th BS. On a few aircraft there were tomahawk silhouettes, representing missions flown by the 93rd Bomb Squadron, 917th Wing, AFRC. *B-52H images by Greg L. Davis*

'HOTSTUFF – ONE DROP IS ALL IT TAKES! – LOUISIANA FIRE' – 96th BS

'CHEROKEE STRIP II' – 93rd BS

KC-135R

'Holy Terror III – LET'S ROLL!'. *Bob Archer*

'OVER 40 And still fuellin' FREEDOM'. *Andreas Hunold*

UNITED STATES NAVY

F-14D of VF-2 'Bounty Hunters'. *US Navy*

F-14B of VF-32 'Swordsmen'. *US Navy*

'GIVE'EM HELL!' - F/A-18C of VFA-105 'Gunslingers'. *Tony Holmes*

F/A-18C of VFA-105 'Gunslingers'. *Tony Holmes*

HIJACK THIS !!!

F/A-18E of VFA-115 'Eagles'. *US Navy*

F/A-18E of VFA-115 'Eagles'. *US Navy*

'GIVE 'EM HELL' - EA-6B of VAQ-130 'Zappers'. *Tony Holmes*

"Give 'em Hell!" 'Give 'em Hell!' - E-2C of VAW-126 'Seahawks'. *Tony Holmes*

CH-46D of HC-11 attached to the USS *Abraham Lincoln* (CVN-72) battle group. *US Navy*

ROYAL AIR FORCE

Tornado GR4/4A

Based at Ali al Salem, Kuwait and Al Udeid, Qatar.

ZA589/DN – 'Deadly Nightshade'. *No IX(B) Sqn*

ZA560/BC – 'BENROMACH'
and 'BRAVE COQ'.
No 12(B) Sqn

ZA592/BJ. *Jamie Hunter/aviacom*

ZA554/BF –
'BORN FIGHTER'.
No 12(B) Sqn

ZA606/BD - 'Big Deal'. *Jamie Hunter/aviacom*

ZA607/AB - 'Delightful Debs'. *Jamie Hunter/aviacom*

ZA607/AB - 'Make all Sure' -
'We are one' (additional art).
Peter J. Cooper/Falcon

ZA542/DM – 'DALLAS DHU' –
'DANGER MOUSE' –
"Crumbs Chief".
Jamie Hunter/aviacom

ZA614/AJ-J - 'It's Showtime'. *Jamie Hunter/aviacom*

ZA600/AJ-L - 'HOT STUFF'.
No 12(B) Sqn

ZD715/AM -
'ALARM MAIDEN'.
No 12(B) Sqn

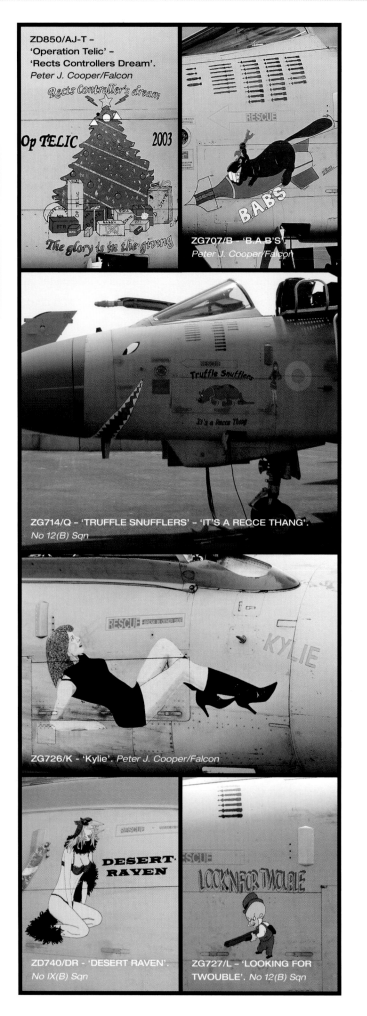

ZD850/AJ-T – 'Operation Telic' – 'Rects Controllers Dream'. *Peter J. Cooper/Falcon*

ZG707/B - 'B.A.B'S'. *Peter J. Cooper/Falcon*

ZG714/Q – 'TRUFFLE SNUFFLERS' – 'IT'S A RECCE THANG'. *No 12(B) Sqn*

ZG726/K – 'Kylie'. *Peter J. Cooper/Falcon*

ZD740/DR - 'DESERT RAVEN'. *No IX(B) Sqn*

ZG727/L – 'LOOKING FOR TWOUBLE'. *No 12(B) Sqn*

Tornado GR4/4A

At the end of the conflict eight GR4/4As remained in theatre at Ali al Salem, Kuwait. These included:

ZA400/T - 'Scud Hunters' – 'Go get 'em Boys!'. *No IX(B) Sqn*

ZA547/DC - 'STAR TURN'. *Denis J. Calvert/Inter-Air Press*

ZA553/DI - 'DISHY INTEL'. *Denis J. Calvert/Inter-Air Press*

ZG711/O - 'OH NELL!'. *Denis J. Calvert/Inter-Air Press*

ZG729/M – 'Mean One' – 'IT'S A GRINCH THING YOU WOULDN'T UNDERSTAND!'. *Denis J. Calvert/Inter-Air Press*

ZG775/FB 'Fat Boy' – 'Macallan'. *No 12(B) Sqn*

Tornado GR4/4A – other aircraft deployed

ZG792/AJ-G	ZD714/AJ-W	'Johnny Walker'
ZA449/AJ-N 'STRATHISLA'	ZD720/TA	'TALISKER'
ZA559/AD 'ABERLOUR'	ZD793/TB	'TAMDHU'
ZA608/TN	ZG777/TC	'CRAIGELLACHIE'
ZA611/TK	ZG794/F	'GLENFARCLAS'

Harrier GR7

Based at Ahmed al Jaber, Kuwait and Azraq, Jordan.

ZG504/75. *RAF Cottesmore*

ZG479/69. *Jamie Hunter/aviacom*

ZD408/37. *Peter J. Cooper/Falcon*

Tornado F3

Prince Sultan AB, Saudi Arabia.

ZE161/UU - '43 OP TELIC 2003'. *Mark McEwan*

ZE161/UU - 'LACEY 28'. *Mark McEwan*

ZE737/YM - 'THE DODGER' - 'STANFORD-TUCK 28'. *Mark McEwan*

ZE758/YI - 'TREMBLE' - 'CALDWELL 28'. *Fighter Foto*

ZE962/XC - 'DENNIS THE MENACE' - 'DEERE 27'. *Fighter Foto*

ZE731/YP – 'BISHOP 72' – 'DESPERATE DAN'. *Mark McEwan*

ZE206/UI – 'Soccer am' – 'Tracy Shaw Thing' – 'BADER 22'. *Fighter Foto*

Canberra PR9, No 39(1 PRU) Sqn
Based at Azraq, Jordan.

XH135. *Peter J. Cooper/Falcon*

XH168 – 'Eastern Promise'. *Peter J. Cooper/Falcon*

XH169 – 'Persian Princess'.
Peter J. Cooper/Falcon

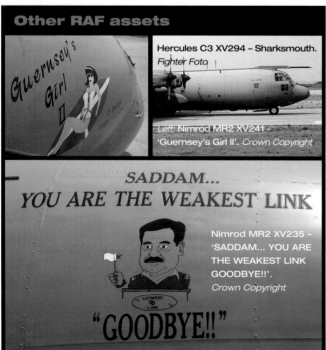

Other RAF assets

Hercules C3 XV294 – Sharksmouth.
Fighter Foto

Left: Nimrod MR2 XV241 –
'Guernsey's Girl II'. *Crown Copyright*

SADDAM...
YOU ARE THE WEAKEST LINK

Nimrod MR2 XV235 –
'SADDAM... YOU ARE
THE WEAKEST LINK
GOODBYE!!'.
Crown Copyright

"GOODBYE!!"

Chinook HC2 – 'COPENHAGEN'.
Jeremy Flack/API

ARMY AIR CORPS/ROYAL MARINES

Lynx AH7

XZ171, 662 Squadron, AAC.
Jeremy Flack/API

XZ617, 847 NAS, Royal Marines.
Peter Cooper/Falcon

XZ208, 847 NAS, Royal Marines.
Peter J. Cooper/Falcon

Coming Home

AMERICA CHANGES FOCUS

As the focus of operations moved from combat operations to the humanitarian future of Iraq, the need for the huge concentration of airpower in the region diminished.

The USAF had already relieved some aircraft, with types such as F-15Cs, F-117As and B-2A Spirits heading out of the region after a job well done. These platforms had fulfilled vital roles in the early days of the campaign, but as Air Supremacy had been established and operations moved towards Close Air Support (CAS), these types made way for more suitable aircraft as battlefield priorities changed.

The US Navy quickly ordered the USS *Kitty Hawk* (CV-63) to return to its base at Yokosuka, Japan, while the USS *Constellation* (CV-64) headed back towards San Diego, CA, having triumphantly completed its last ever cruise before decommissioning. The USS *Abraham Lincoln* (CVN-72) had already been relieved by the USS *Nimitz* (CVN-68), and was heading back to Everett, WA, in late April 2003.

Forces remaining in theatre were tasked with tackling small pockets of resistance, with US Army battlefield support helicopters remaining extremely busy.

The extensive US Marine Corps deployment was also scaled down, with the amphibious assault ships heading back to port to be replaced in theatre by fresh assets. Members of VMA-211 returned home with the USS *Bonhomme Richard* (LHD-6) in May 2003. The unit flew approximately 600 missions during OIF according to Maj Chris Kyler, its operations officer. 'We did all of it out there; CAS, recon' missions and aerial interdiction'. Harrier pilot Capt Scott Luckie added; 'It's just great to be home'.

Top: **Job well done. US Navy F/A-18C Hornet pilots from VFA-192 'World Famous Golden Dragons' arrive back at NAF Atsugi, Japan, having been heavily involved in OIF.** *US Navy*

Above: **B-1B Lancers of the 37th BS are welcomed back to Ellsworth AFB, SD, on 13 May 2003 as they return from OIF. As of 8 May the B-1s had flown an impressive 497 combat missions supporting both OIF, and Operation 'Enduring Freedom' over Afghanistan.** *USAF*

Left: **Three female USAF fast-jet crewmembers assigned to the 379th AEW at Al Udeid, Qatar, prepare to head home after a successful campaign.** *USAF*

Below: **A gaggle of F-15C Eagles from the 1st FW arrives back at Langley AFB, VA. The Eagles quickly gained total air supremacy over Iraq, with the Iraqi AF staying on the ground.** *USAF*

Above: Col Steve Miller, Commander of the 1st FW at Langley AFB, VA, greets a 49th FW F-117A pilot as the Stealth Fighters stage through the base en-route back to Holloman AFB, NM, on 14 April 2003. *USAF*

Below: A USAF E-3 Sentry of the 552nd Air Control Wing gets hosed down by the fire department as it arrives back at Tinker AFB, OK, on 28 April 2003. *USAF*

Bottom: 'Swamp Foxes' head home. A pilot from the 157th EFS prepares to return to South Carolina. *USAF*

Top right: A C-130H of the 181st AS, Oklahoma ANG, seen staging through RAF Akrotiri, Cyprus, on the way back home. *Fighter Foto*

Right: Back at Spangdahlem, Germany, after a successful OIF deployment, the 22nd FS 'Stingers' F-16CJs got straight back into the training regime that prepared them so well for combat over Iraq. *Jamie Hunter/aviacom*

HOLLOMAN'S HEROES

Once back at Holloman AFB, NM, the F-117A Nighthawks of the 49th FW got straight back into the rigorous training schedule that had prepared them so well for OIF. These pictures were taken soon after the Stealth Fighters had returned from combat.

Above: In its 'Canyon' at Holloman AFB, NM, an F-117A Nighthawk is prepared for a night training mission. *Jamie Hunter/aviacom*

Right: A Nighthawk pilot goes through his pre-taxi checks at the start of a mission from Holloman. *Jamie Hunter/aviacom*

Below: Swathed in golden early evening light, a 49th FW F-117A taxies out of its 'Canyon'. *Jamie Hunter/aviacom*

Left: Cruising above the White Sands National Monument and missile test range, this F-117A is lit up by the bright desert below. *Jamie Hunter/aviacom*

Below left: Pitching out – the F-117A is a fairly nimble aircraft as illustrated here. *Jamie Hunter/aviacom*

Below: Banking over White Sands, a pair of 'One-Seventeens' (radio callsign 'Geiger 1 and 2') break away from the T-38 cameraship. *Jamie Hunter/aviacom*

Bottom: As the sun sets into a shimmering haze, the F-117A comes into its own. In the words of the F-117 pilots – 'we own the night' and OIF proved it once again. *Jamie Hunter/aviacom*

BRITISH HEAD HOME

The UK Ministry of Defence announced that forces in the region would start being reduced almost immediately after the cessation of the 'air war'. HMS *Ark Royal* returned to the UK for its 'air wing to be re-generated' while various RAF assets were welcomed back throughout April 2003.

The Tornado F3 detachment from Prince Sultan AB in Saudi Arabia was the first RAF deployment to return to the UK. The crews had come under fire several times and are thought to have taken part in around 1,000 hours of flying during the combat phase of Operation 'Telic'. On 11 April, the first Tornado F3s, crewed by No 111 Squadron, arrived back at RAF Leuchars to be greeted by family members and well-wishers.

On 17 April, the first RAF Tornado GR4 personnel started returning home from the Gulf. A small party of 28 air and ground crews from No 617 Squadron 'Dambusters' returned to RAF Lossiemouth after flying into Glasgow on board a civilian flight. They were the first to return to 'Lossie' from a total of 500 personnel deployed from the base.

Squadron 'boss' Wg Cdr Dave Robertson and the crews of No 617 Squadron had been the first to use the new MBDA Storm Shadow cruise missile, with the squadron undertaking precision attacks on Iraqi command and control bunkers in and around Baghdad. 'It was absolutely incredible', remarked Wg Cdr Robertson upon his return to British soil. 'It was totally amazing and something that will live with me for the rest of my life'.

Top left: **High above the Mediterranean en-route back home to RAF Marham, this immaculate four-ship formation of Tornado GR4s are crewed by No IX(B) Squadron.** *Jamie Hunter/aviacom*

Above: **Good job! Tornado GR4 pilot and navigator shake hands upon their return to RAF Marham at the completion of the combat phase of Operation 'Telic'.** *Richard Cooper*

Inset: **Good to be back. A Harrier GR7 pilot waves to waiting friends and family upon returning to RAF Cottesmore.** *Richard Cooper*

The remaining Tornado GR4 contingent returned to a heroes welcome on 6 May 2003 as No IX(B) Squadron, led by Wg Cdr Derek Watson, flew back to RAF Marham from Ali al Salem.

The first RAF Harrier GR7s returned to RAF Cottesmore from the Gulf on Friday 18 April 2003. The nine GR7s from No 3 Squadron were led back home by Wg Cdr Stuart Atha. He said: 'We are extremely happy and relieved to be back. They have done a tremendous job out there and we can be very proud of them'. Wg Cdr Rob Adlam, who was the base commander for the 'Det' said: 'They did their last operation on Tuesday and since then the base has just been on a sense of high excitement'. The Harrier pilots had been in theatre since 9 March 2003 and had flown several hundred missions over Iraqi during Operation 'Telic'. Wg Cdr Atha added: 'I don't think anyone expected it to turn out the way it did. It was a lot quicker than any of us expected. We were only out there for

Left: **Returning back home to the No IX(B) Squadron flightline at RAF Marham on 6 May 2003, these RAF Tornado GR4s were deployed to Ali al Salem, Kuwait, for Operation 'Telic'.** *Richard Cooper*

Right: **Royal Marines Lynx AH7s of 847NAS return to RNAS Yeovilton at the successful completion of their deployment for Operation 'Telic' aboard HMS *Ocean*.** *Peter J. Cooper/Falcon Aviation Photographs*

seven weeks, which is nothing compared to some of the guys. We have been very fortunate, some of them are going to have to be there for some time'. Reflecting on the missions, Wg Cdr Atha said: 'The worst part was just before we went up, especially the first night. We did not know what to expect. It was the fear of the unknown. When you are up there you feel a mix of emotions, there are times when you are scared, but most of the time you are concerned with just doing a good job'.

A second contingent of Harriers from Ahmed al Jaber returned on 7 May 2003 to RAF Cottesmore. These aircraft were flown by No IV(AC) Squadron crews and staged home via RAF Akrotiri, Cyprus. A number of No 1(F) Squadron crews remained in theatre to fulfil reconnaissance duties over Iraq in support of those Coalition forces still deployed.

TORNADO ACES

As Royal Air Force Tornado GR4/4As returned to the UK at the end of the combat phase of Operation 'Telic', squadron personnel were quickly back practising the wide range of skills that enabled the Tornado and its ace crews to adapt to so many tasks over Iraq.

Above: Blasting through the remote Scottish valleys, a Tornado GR4A, still wearing its temporary light grey warpaint, is flown by a No 617 Squadron crew (with Flt Lt Andy Turk as Navigator – see Foreword). The crews constantly maintain proficiency in the important low-level role. *Jamie Hunter/aviacom*

Left: A 'Dambusters' GR4 tucks its undercarriage as it heads out for a training mission from RAF Lossiemouth. *Richard Cooper*

Left: The RAF Tornado GR4s soon lost their temporary light grey finish, however, many retained nose art for some weeks after returning from the Gulf. This example is ZA600/AJ-L – 'HOT STUFF'. *Jamie Hunter/aviacom*

Top right: This Tornado GR4 of No 12(B) Squadron is flown by Sqn Ldr 'D-L'. He flew combat missions over Iraq during Operation 'Telic'. *Richard Cooper*

Inset: A pair of GR4s from No 12(B) Squadron practice formation skills at low-level on a training mission from RAF Lossiemouth. *Jamie Hunter/aviacom*

Right: 'Pointy wing' – a Tornado GR4 heads for its next 'target' during a training mission. As soon as the crews returned from the Gulf, the training programme resumed. *Jamie Hunter/aviacom*

Appendix 1

US MILITARY OPERATION 'IRAQI FREEDOM' FLYING UNITS

US AIR FORCE

363rd Air Expeditionary Wing
Prince Sultan AB, Saudi Arabia

58th FS 'Gorillas'	F-15C	EG
67th FS 'Fighting Cocks'	5x F-15C	ZZ
14th FS 'Samurais'	18x F-16CG/DG	WW
457th FS 'Spads'	6x F-16C [a]	TX
363rd Expeditionary AACS	6x E-3B/C	OK
116th ACW	E-8C J-STARS	WR/GA
38th RS	4x RC-135V/W	OF
363rd ERS	2x U-2S	BB
92nd ARW	17x KC-135R/T	

384th Air Expeditionary Wing
Tabuk, Saudi Arabia

916th ARS	KC-135R

332nd Air Expeditionary Group
Al Jaber AB, Kuwait

172nd FS 'Mad Ducks'	OA/A-10A	BC
190th FS	OA/A-10A	ID
303rd FS 'KC Hawgs'	OA/A-10A	KC
23rd FG	OA/A-10A	FT
104th FS 'Fighting Orioles'	OA/A-10A	MD
524th FS 'Hounds'	18x F-16CG	CC
39th RQS	HC-130/C-130E	
301st RQS	HH-60G	

386th Air Expeditionary Wing
Ali Al Salem AB, Kuwait

38th RQS	HH-60G	
939 RQW	HC-130P	
20th SOS	MH-53M	
8th SOS	MC-130E	
15th RS	RQ/MQ-1	WA

320th Air Expeditionary Group
Seeb, Oman

778th Expeditionary AS	C-130
189th AS	C-130E

405th Air Expeditionary Wing
Thumrait, Oman

34th BS 'Thunderbirds'	B-1B	EL
37th BS 'Tigers'	B-1B	EL
552nd ACW	4x E-3	OK
	KC-135R	

379th Air Expeditionary Wing
Al Udeid AB, Qatar

8th EFS 'Black Sheep'	12x F-117A	HO
4th FW	48x F-15E	SJ
22nd EFS 'Stingers'	12x F-16CJ/DJ	SP
157th EFS 'Swamp Foxes'	F-16CJ	
379th Expeditionary ARS	KC-10A	
44th Expeditionary ARS	KC-10A	
340th Expeditionary ARS	KC-135R	
911th ARS	KC-135R	
434th ARW	KC-135R	
1st AS	C-40A	

380th Air Expeditionary Wing
Al Dhafra AB, UAE

9th RW, Det 4	U-2S	BB
12th RS	RQ-4A	
763rd Expeditionary ARS	KC-10A	
908th Expeditionary ARS	KC-10A	
193rd SOW	EC-130E	
41st ECS 'Scorpions'	EC-130H	DM

358th Air Expeditionary Wing
Sheikh Isa, Bahrain

71st FS 'Ironmen'	F-15C	FF
—	C-130	

410th Air Expeditionary Wing
Azraq, Jordan

118th FS 'Flying Yankees'	A/OA-10A	CT
77th FS 'Gamblers'	F-16CJ	SW
120th FS 'Cougars'	F-16C	CO
160th FS 'Snakes'	F-16C	AL
71st RQS 'Kings'	HC-130P	
66th RQS	HH-60G	
4th SOS	AC-130U	
8th SOS	MC-130E	
20th SOS	MH-53M	
15th RS	MQ/RQ-1	WA

392nd Air Expeditionary Wing
Tallil, Iraq

—	A-10A/AV-8B	
301st RQS	HH-60G	

40th Air Expeditionary Wing
Diego Garcia, Indian Ocean

393rd BS 'Tigers'	B-2A	WM
20th EBS 'Buccaneers'	B-52H	LA
40th EBS	B-52H	LA
462nd Air Expeditionary Group	KC-135R	

398th Air Expeditionary Wing
Souda Bay, Crete

55th RW	RC-135W	OF
412th TW	NKC-135E	
	KC-135R	

401st Air Expeditionary Wing
RAF Akrotiri, Cyprus

—	36x KC-135R	
116th ACW	2x E-8C	WR/GA
552nd ACW	3x E-3	OK
99th EARS	U-2S	BB

457th Air Expeditionary Group
RAF Fairford, UK

23rd BS 'Bomber Barons'	B-52H	MT
93rd BS 'Indian Outlaws'	B-52H	BD

409th Air Expeditionary Group
Bourgas, Bulgaria

—	KC-10A

458th Air Expeditionary Group

—	C-130

US NAVY
Mediterranean Sea

USS Harry S. Truman (CVN-75)

CVW-3 'AC'

VF-32 'Swordsmen'	F-14B
VFA-37 'Bulls'	F/A-18C
VFA-105 'Gunslingers'	F/A-18C
VMFA-115 'Silver Eagles'	F/A-18A+
VAW-126 'Seahawks'	E-2C
VAQ-130 'Zappers'	EA-6B
VS-22 'Checkmates'	S-3B
HS-7 'Dusty Dogs'	SH-60F/HH-60H
VRC-40 'Rawhides' Det 1	C-2A

USS Theodore Roosevelt (CVN-71)

CVW-8 'AJ'

VF-213 'Blacklions'	F-14D
VFA-15 'Valions'	F/A-18C
VFA-87 'Golden Warriors'	F/A-18C
VFA-201 'Hunters'	F/A-18A+
VAW-124 'Bear Aces'	E-2C
VAQ-141 'Shadowhawks'	EA-6B
VS-24 'Scouts'	S-3B
HS-3 'Tridents'	SH-60F/HH-60H
VRC-40 'Rawhides' Det 5	C-2A

US NAVY
Northern Arabian Gulf (NAG)

USS Kitty Hawk (CV-63)

CVW-5 'NF'

VF-154 'Black Knights'	F-14A
VFA-27 'Royal Maces'	F/A-18C
VFA-192 'World Famous Golden Dragons'	F/A-18C
VFA-195 'Dambusters'	F/A-18C
VAW-115 'Liberty Bells'	E-2C
VAQ-136 'Gauntlets'	EA-6B
VS-21 'Fighting Redtails'	S-3B
HS-14 'Chargers'	SH-60F/HH-60H
VRC-30 'Providers' Det 5	C-2A

USS Constellation (CV-64)

CVW-2 'NE'

VF-2 'Bounty Hunters'	F-14D
VFA-137 'Kestrels'	F/A-18C
VFA-151 'Vigilantes'	F/A-18C
VMFA-323 'Death Rattlers'	F/A-18C
VAQ-131 'Lancers'	EA-6B

Continued...

Below: The USAF's 379th AEW at Al Udeid got together with fellow deployed Coalition assets for this unique shot taken at the base. The picture features an 8th EFS 'Black Sheep' F-117A, 4th FW F-15Es, a 22nd EFS 'Stingers' F-16CJ, a 157th EFS 'Swamp Foxes' F-16CJ, a KC-135R, a 1st AS C-40A, a C-20, a C-21A, an HH-60G, as well as RAF Tornado GR4 and 125 CC3 and an RAAF F/A-18A Hornet. *USAF*

Left: Led by an A-10A of 172nd FS 'Mad Ducks', representatives from the deployed squadrons at Al Jaber, Kuwait, formate over the base. Other aircraft in the formation are a US Marine Corps F/A-18C of VMFA-251 'Thunderbolts', a VMA-214 'Black Sheep' AV-8B+, a 524th FS 'Hounds' F-16CG and an RAF Harrier GR7. Note that most of the aircraft carry live weapons. *via No 1(F) Squadron*

USS *Constellation* (CV-64) (NAG operations) *continued*

VAW-116 'Sun Kings'	E-2C
VS-38 'Red Griffins'	S-3B
HS-2 'Golden Falcons'	SH-60F/HH-60H
VRC-30 'Providers' Det 2	C-2A

USS *Abraham Lincoln* (CVN-72)

CVW-14 'NK'

VF-31 'Tomcatters'	F-14D
VFA-25 'Fist of the Fleet'	F/A-18C
VFA-113 'Stingers'	F/A-18C
VFA-115 'Eagles'	F/A-18E
VAW-113 'Black Eagles'	E-2C
VAQ-139 'Cougars'	EA-6B
VS-35 'Blue Wolves'	S-3B
HS-4 'Black Knights'	SH-60F/HH-60H
VRC-30 'Providers' Det 1	C-2A

USS *Nimitz* (CVN-68)

CVW-11 'NH'

VFA-14 'Tophatters'	F/A-18E
VFA-41 'Black Aces'	F/A-18F
VFA-94 'Mighty Shrikes'	F/A-18C
VFA-97 'Warhawks'	F/A-18A
VAW-117 'Wallbangers'	E-2C
VAQ-135 'Black Ravens'	EA-6B
VS-29 'Dragonfires'	S-3B
HS-6 'Indians'	SH-60F/HH-60H
VRC-30 'Providers' Det 3	C-2A

Land-based

HM-15 'Blackhawks'	MH-53E	
VP-1 'Screaming Eagles'	P-3C (AIP)	Ali al Salem/ Muharraq
VP-40 'Fighting Marlins'	P-3C (AIP)	
VP-46 'Gray Knights'	P-3C (AIP)	
VP-47 'Golden Swordsmen'	P-3C (AIP)	Ali al Salem
VQ-1 'World Watchers'	EP-3E ARIES II	Muharraq
VQ-2 'Batmen'	EP-3E ARIES II	Souda Bay
HC-2 Det 2 'Desert Ducks'	UH-3H	Muharraq
HC-4 'Black Stallions'	MH-53E	Akrotiri/ Muharraq
VAQ-142 'Gray Wolves'	EA-6B	Prince Sultan AB
—	UC-12M	

US MARINE CORPS

Amphibious Task Force (West)

USS *Tarawa* (LHA-1)
USS *Bonhomme Richard* (LHD-6)
3rd Marine Aircraft Wing, Marine Aircraft Group 13

USS *Tarawa* (LHA-1)

HMM-161 'Greyhawks'	12x CH-46E
	4x CH-53E
	3x UH-1N
	4x AH-1W
VMA-311 'Tomcats'	AV-8B+

USS *Bonhomme Richard* (LHD-6)

HMM-263 'Thunder Chickens'	12x CH-46E
	4x CH-53E
	3x UH-1N
	4x AH-1W
VMA-211 'Avengers'	AV-8B+

Amphibious Task Force (East)

**USS *Saipan* (LHA-2), USS *Nassau* (LHA-4),
USS *Kearsarge* (LHD-3), USS *Bataan* (LHD-5)**
Marine Aircraft Group 29

HMM-162 'Golden Eagles'	CH-46E
HMM-365 'Sky Knights'	CH-46E
HMH-464 'Condors'	CH-53E
HMLA-269 'Gunrunners'	UH-1N/AH-1W
VMA-223 'Bulldogs'	AV-8B+
VMA-542 'Flying Tigers' (land-based at Ahmed al Jaber)	AV-8B+

Land-based

VMFA(AW)-121 'Green Knights'	F/A-18D	Ahmed al Jaber
VMFA-232 'Red Devils'	F/A-18C	Ahmed al Jaber
VMFA-251 'Thunderbolts'	F/A-18C	Ahmed al Jaber
VMFA(AW)-225 'Vikings'	F/A-18D	Ahmed al Jaber
VMFA(AW)-533 'Hawks'	F/A-18D	Ahmed al Jaber
VMA-214 'Black Sheep'	AV-8B+	Ahmed al Jaber
VMA-542 'Flying Tigers'	AV-8B+	Ahmed al Jaber
VMGR-452 'Yankees'	KC-130T	Sheikh Isa
—	KC-130T	Ali al Salem
VMAQ-1 'Screaming Banshees'	EA-6B	Prince Sultan AB
VMAQ-2 'Death Jesters'	EA-6B	Prince Sultan AB

US ARMY

1st Armored Division
1st Infantry Division
1st Cavalry Division

3rd BN, 158th Aviation Regt	UH-60L
5th BN, 158th Aviation Regt	UH-60A

11th Aviation Regt
3rd Infantry Division
4th Infantry Division – Mechanized
82nd Airborne Division
101st Airborne Division

1st BN, 101st Aviation Regt	AH-64D
2nd BN, 101st Aviation Regt	AH-64D
3rd BN, 101st Aviation Regt	AH-64A
6th BN, 101st Aviation Regt	UH-60A/UH-60L

Task Force Ironhorse

BRITISH MILITARY OPERATION 'TELIC' FLYING UNITS

ROYAL AIR FORCE

RAF Akrotiri, Cyprus

No 10 Squadron	VC10 C1K (Medevac)

Prince Sultan AB, Saudi Arabia

No 8/23 Squadron	E-3D
No 32(TR) Squadron	125 CC3
No 51 Squadron	Nimrod R1
No 10, 101 Squadron	VC10
Nos 43(F), 111(F) Squadron	Tornado F3
No 120, 201, 206 Squadron	Nimrod MR2

Ali al Salem AB, Kuwait

Nos II(AC), IX(B), XIII, 31, 617 Squadrons	Tornado GR4/4A
No 18 Squadron	Chinook HC2
No 33 Squadron	Puma HC1

Ahmed al Jaber AB, Kuwait

Nos 1(F), IV(AC) Squadrons	Harrier GR7

Muharraq, Bahrain

No 216 Squadron	TriStar KC1

Al Udeid AB, Qatar

Nos II(AC), 12(B), 617 Squadrons	Tornado GR4/4A
No 32(TR) Squadron	125 CC3

Azraq, Jordan

No 3 Squadron	Harrier GR7
No 39(1 PRU) Squadron	Canberra PR9

Seeb, Oman

No 120, 201, 206 Squadron	Nimrod MR2

HMS Ark Royal

No 18 Squadron	Chinook HC2

ROYAL NAVY

HMS Ark Royal

849NAS, A Flt	Sea King ASaC7

HMS Ocean

845NAS	Sea King HC4
847NAS	Gazelle AH1/Lynx AH7

RFA Fort Victoria

814NAS	Merlin HM1

RFA Argus, Rosalie

820NAS	Sea King HAS6

HMS Cardiff, Chatham, Edinburgh, Liverpool, Marlborough, Richmond, York

815NAS	Lynx HAS3S/HMA8

BRITISH ARMY AIR CORPS

Ali al Salem/Forward Operating Bases

3 Regiment	Gazelle AH1/Lynx AH7

AUSTRALIAN MILITARY OPERATION 'FALCONER' FLYING UNITS

ROYAL AUSTRALIAN AIR FORCE

Al Udeid AB, Qatar

No 75 Squadron	F/A-18A HUG
92 Wing	P-3C
No 36, 37 Squadrons	C-130H/J

Azraq, Jordan

5th Regiment	CH-47D

ROYAL AUSTRALIAN NAVY

HMAS Anzac ('Akubra' flight)	S-70B
HMAS Darwin ('Agro' flight)	S-70B
HMAS Kanimbla ('Shark' flight)	Sea King Mk50A

Appendix 2

OIF FACTS AND FIGURES

Figures are based on US military releases at the end of the official combat phase and do not include regular US Army assets.

OIF AIRCRAFT

Total Aircraft	**1,801**
US Air Force	**863**
Fighters	293
Bombers	51
C2	22
Tankers	182
ISR	60
Special Ops/Rescue	58
Airlift	111
SOF	73
Other	13
US Navy	**408**
Fighters	232
C2	20
Tankers	52
ISR	29
Airlift	5
Other	70
US Marine Corps	**372**
Fighters	130
Tankers	22
Other	220
Royal Air Force	**113**
Fighters	66
C2	4
ISR	9
Tankers	12
Special Ops/Rescue	14
Airlift	4
Other	4
Royal Australian AF	**22**
Fighters	14
ISR	2
Airlift	3
Other	3

Right: The Boeing F/A-18 Hornet was the most numerous type deployed for OIF, with the US Navy, US Navy Reserve, US Marine Corps and Royal Australian AF sending over 250 examples. The weapon of choice throughout the campaign was the GBU-31 JDAM, with over 5,000 dropped. This Hornet carries one JDAM, two GBU-12 LGBs, plus two AIM-9s, an AIM-120 and a targeting pod. *US Navy*

US AIR FORCE RESERVE AIRCRAFT

Total Aircraft	**70**
A/OA-10A	12
F-16	6
KC-135	22
C-130	6
B-52H	6
MC-130P	6
HC-130	4
HH-60	6

USAF AIR NATIONAL GUARD AIRCRAFT

Total Aircraft	**236**
A/OA-10A	47
F-16	45
KC-135	57
C-130	72
E-8C	9
MC-130P	2
EC-130E	1
HH-60	3

PSYCOLOGICAL OPERATIONS (PSYOPS)

Leaflets Dropped	31,800,000
Leaflet Missions	158
(A-10A Leaflet Missions	32)
(B-52H Leaflet Missions	34)
(F/A-18C Leaflet Missions	24)
(F-16CJ Leaflet Missions	68)
EC-130E Commando Solo Sorties	58
EC-130H Compass Call Sorties	125

TOTAL PERSONNEL DEPLOYED

US Air Force	54,955
(Reserve	2,084)
(National Guard	7,207)
US Navy	61,296
(Reserve	2,056)
US Marine Corps	74,405
(Reserve	9,501)
British	40,906
Australian	2,050
Canadian	31

MUNITIONS EXPENDED

Guided Munitions	19,948		
BGM-109 TLAM	802	GBU-32 JDAM	768
AGM-114 Hellfire	562	GBU-35 JDAM	675
AGM-130	4	GBU-37 JDAM	13
AGM-154 JSOW	253	Paveway/Enhanced Paveway II/III	679
AGM-65 Maverick	918		
AGM-84 SLAM(ER)	3		
AGM-86C/D CALCM	153	**Unguided Munitions**	**9,251**
AGM-88 HARM	408	M117	1,625
CBU-103 WCMD	818	Mk82	5,504
CBU-105 WCMD	88	Mk83	1,692
CBU-107 WCMD	2	Mk84	6
EGBU-27 GPS/LGB	98	CBU-87	118
GBU-10 LGB	236	CBU-99	182
GBU-12 LGB	7,114	UK Unguided	124
GBU-16 LGB	1,233	Ammunition	328,498
GBU-24 LGB	23	(20mm	16,901)
GBU-27 LGB	11	(30mm	311,597)
GBU-28 LGB	1	Leaflet Dispensers	348
GBU-31 JDAM	5,086	(PDU-5	44)
		(M129	304)

ENEMY RESPONSES

AAA (Triple A) events (reported via MISREP)	1,224
SAM/Rocket launches (reported via MISREP)	1,660
SAM Emitters active (reported via MISREP)	436
SSM launches	19

SIGNIFICANT OIF COMBAT FIRSTS

United States Air Force

- B-1B used Moving Target Indicator (MTI) for ISR.
- B-2A employed Mk82 bombs.
- B-52H used of Litening II targeting pod to designate Laser Guided Bombs.
- B-52H CALCM/JDAM mixed load operations.
- First combat package to include B-1Bs, B-2As, and B-52Hs.
- C-17As used for Combat Personnel Drop.
- EC-130H Compass Call used in PSYOPS role.
- RQ-4 Global Hawk used for SCAR (Strike Co-ordination And Reconnaissance).
- Six U-2S flew joint mission in support of one Air Tasking Order.
- Employment of CBU-105 Wind Corrected Munitions Dispenser.
- Employment of AGM-86D penetrating CALCM.

US Navy

- F-14D employed GBU-31 JDAM.
- EA-6B used in PSYOPS role.
- F/A-18E/F widespread conflict (and F used in tanker role).

US Army

- Combat use of AH-64D Apache Longbow.

Royal Air Force

- Combat use of MBDA Storm Shadow stand-off cruise missile.

AIRCRAFT TYPE TOTALS (Deployed for OIF)

Aircraft	Total	Aircraft	Total
A/OA-10A Thunderbolt II	60	Harrier GR7	18
AC-130U/H Spooky/Spectre	8	HC-130H/P Hercules	8
AH-1 Cobra (various)	58	HH-60H/G Pave Hawk	16
AH-6J 'Little Bird'	8	HS125 CC3	3
AV-8B Harrier II	70	KC-10A Extender	33
B-1B Lancer	11	KC-130 Hercules	22
B-2A Spirit (plus 8 from Whiteman AFB)	4	KC-135E/R Stratotanker	149
B-52H Stratofortress	28	Lynx AH7/HAS3S/HMA8	25
Canberra PR9	2	MC-130E/H Combat Talon	26
Chinook HC2	11	Merlin HM1	4
C-130 Hercules (various)	124	MH-47E Chinook	14
C-17A Globemaster III	7	MH-53M Pave Low IV	31
C-2A Greyhound	10	MH-6J 'Little Bird'	7
C-20 (various)	3	MH-60L/G Black Hawk	18
C-21A	7	MQ-1L Predator	7
C-32A	1	Nimrod MR2	6
C-40A Clipper	1	Nimrod R1	1
C-9A Nightingale	5	NKC-135E Big Crow	1
CH-46E Sea Knight	67	P-3C Orion	28
CH-53E Sea Stallion	54	Puma HC1	7
CN-235	1	RC-12 (various)	18
DC-130A Hercules	1	RC-135V/W Rivet Joint	9
E-2C Hawkeye	20	RQ-1A Predator	9
E-3B/C/D AWACS/Sentry	19	RQ-4A Global Hawk	1
E-8C J-STARS	9	S-3B Viking	40
EA-6B Prowler	35	S-70B-2 Seahawk	2
EC-130E/H Hercules	8	Sea King HC4/ASaC7/HAS6	20
EP-3E ARIES II	3	Sea King Mk50A	1
F/A-18A/A+/C/D/E/F Hornet & Super Hornet	250	Tornado F3	14
F-117A Nighthawk	12	Tornado GR4/4A	30
F-14A/B/D Tomcat	56	TriStar KC1	4
F-15C Eagle	42	U-2S Dragonlady	15
F-15E Strike Eagle	48	UC-12M	3
F-16A/C Fighting Falcon	60	UH-1 Huey (various)	30
F-16CJ Fighting Falcon	71	UH-3H Sea King	4
Gazelle AH1	16	VC10	8

Note: Total does not include regular US Army assets

GLOSSARY

AAA	Anti-Aircraft Artillery, also 'Triple-A'
ACC	Air Combat Command
ACW	Air Control Wing
AEW	Air Expeditionary Wing
AEW	Airborne Early Warning
ALARM	Air-Launched Anti-Radiation Missile
AMC	Air Mobility Command
ARS	Air Refuelling Squadron
ARW	Air Refuelling Wing
AS	Airlift Squadron
ASW	Anti-Submarine Warfare
AWACS	Airborne Warning and Control System
BS	Bomb Squadron
BW	Bomb Wing
C2	Command and Control
DEAD	Destruction of Enemy Air Defences
EFS	Expeditionary Fighter Squadron
EPW	Enhanced Paveway
JDAM	Joint Direct Attack Munition
JSOW	Joint Stand-Off Weapon
J-STARS	Joint Surveillance Target Attack Radar System
FARP	Forward Arming and Refuelling Point
FS	Fighter Squadron
FG	Fighter Group
FW	Fighter Wing
FOL	Forward Operating Location
HARM	High-speed Anti-Radiation Missile
ISR	Intelligence, Surveillance and Reconnaissance
LANTIRN	Low Altitude Navigation and Targeting Infra-Red for Night
LGB	Laser-Guided Bomb
ONW	Operation 'Northern Watch'
OSW	Operation 'Southern Watch'
OIF	Operation 'Iraqi Freedom'
RAPTOR	Reconnaissance Airborne Pod for TORnado
RQS	Rescue Squadron
RQW	Rescue Wing
RS	Reconnaissance Squadron
SAM	Surface-to-Air Missile
SCAR	Strike Co-ordination And Reconnaissance
SEAD	Suppression of Enemy Air Defences
SOF	Special Operations Forces
SOS	Special Operations Squadron
SSM	Surface-to-Surface Missile
TIALD	Thermal Imaging and Airborne Laser Designator
UAV	Unmanned Aerial Vehicle
USAF	United States Air Force
VUL	Vulnerability Time
WCMD	Wind Corrected Munitions Dispenser

MISSIONS (Total Sorties Flown)

US Air Force	24,196	US Navy	8,945
Fighters	8,828	Fighters	5,568
Bombers	505	Tankers	2,058
Tankers	6,193	C2 (E-2C)	442
Airlift	7,413	ISR	357
C2 (E-3B/C and E-8C)	432	Other	520
ISR	452		
Rescue	191	**United Kingdom**	**2,481**
Other	182	Fighters	1,736
		Tankers	359
US Marine Corps	**4,948**	C2 (E-3D)	112
Fighters	3,794	ISR	273
Tankers	454	Other	1
ISR	305		
C2	75	**Australian**	**565**
Other	320	Fighters	302
		Airlift	263

Appendix 3

BATTLE DAMAGE ASSESSMENT

The unprecedented use of high-tech weaponry heralded astonishing results. Coalition commanders also made good use of the latest imagery gathering techniques to monitor the attacks as they happened. This is just a sample of some of the incredible Battle Damage Assessment (BDA) imagery that was released, showing the carefully targeted Coalition attacks.

All photography courtesy of the US Department of Defense unless otherwise stated.

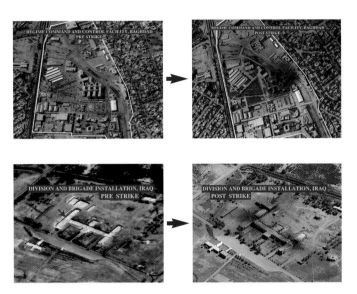

Above: Saddam Hussein's presidential yacht was claimed by a number of airstrikes. It sits here forlornly in Basra harbour having been struck by VF-2 'Bounty Hunters' F-14 Tomcats. *US Navy*

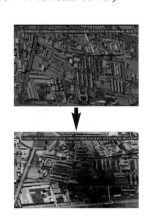

Appendix 4

COMBAT CASUALTIES

20 March 2003

- The opening night of the war saw the first casualty of Operation 'Iraqi Freedom'. A USAF Special Forces MH-53M Pave Low IV crash-landed in unknown circumstances inside Iraq.
- A US Army 11th Aviation Brigade AH-64 made a hard landing inside Iraq. Both helicopter and crew were recovered safely.

21 March

- A US Marine Corps CH-46E Sea Knight crashed in northern Kuwait, killing the eight Royal Marines and four US Marine Corps aircrew on board.

22 March

- Two Royal Navy Sea King ASaC7s of 849NAS collided near HMS *Ark Royal* as one aircraft departed the ship and one recovered for refuelling. Six Royal Navy crewmembers and a US observer were killed in the accident.

23 March

- An RAF Tornado GR4 from the Marham Wing based at Ali al Salem was shot down by a US Patriot missile in a friendly fire accident. The aircraft was reportedly one of a pair returning from a SEAD combat mission over Iraq. Both Flt Lt Kev Main and Flt Lt David Williams from No IX(B) Squadron lost their lives.

BEHIND ENEMY LINES

Tomcat down

A pair of VF-154 'Black Knights' F-14A Tomcats had delivered a precision payload and were returning back to their shore detachment from CVW-5 aboard the USS *Kitty Hawk* (CV-63). As the two jets headed for the tanker, one suffered an engine failure. Once the fuel transfer system failed, the outcome was inevitable. 'We knew what was coming,' the pilot commented. 'I was just counting down the fuel level. When it got down to about 200lb the right engine started to come down, the generator started to hiccup and it was time to go'. There was only one option: 'Eject, eject, eject!'

Having come back down to earth, the pilots got out their global positioning system and charts. It became clear that they had come down over Iraq. 'It was a fairly surreal experience. You go from sitting in the warmth and comfort of your cockpit to a violent windblast and hitting the desert floor pretty hard in your parachute'. However, they were able to quickly alert CSAR forces of their position and were rapidly extracted before they could fall into enemy hands.

24 March

- US Army AH-64D 99-5135 of 11th Aviation Brigade (C Company, 'Vampires', 1-227 Attack Helicopter Battalion, 1st Cavalry Division from Fort Hood, TX), was shown on Iraqi TV having force-landed in a field near Najaf. This Apache was one of around 40 examples that attacked the Medina Division Republican Guard south of Baghdad. The crew was captured by Iraqi forces, but were later found safe and well as the Coalition advanced through Iraq. The AH-64 was later destroyed by a 77th FS F-16CJ.

26 March

- Phoenix UAV, ZJ300, British Army, shot down near Basra.
- Phoenix UAV, ZJ393, British Army, shot down near Basra.

27 March

- USAF RQ-1B Predator UAV (95-014) shot down over Baghdad.

28 March

- The US Army lost two AH-64 Apaches on this date. The AH-64A and AH-64D were part of the 2-101st Avn, 101st Airborne Division 'Screamin' Eagles' and had been flying attack missions against Republican Guard units to the south of Baghdad.

29 March

- A US Army UH-60 crashed in 'brown-out' conditions.
- Two US Army OH-58 Kiowa Warriors of the 11th Aviation Brigade were damaged by small arms fire.

30 March

- A single US Marine Corps AV-8B assigned to HMM-263 crashed whilst attempting to land aboard the USS *Nassau* (LHA-4) at night. The pilot ejected safely and was rescued by a SAR CH-46E.
- A US Marine Corps UH-1N of HMLA-169 crashed near its Forward Operating Base (FOB) near Karbala, killing all three aircrew on board.

1 April

- US Navy S-3B (BuNo 160126) of VS-38 'Red Griffins' from CVW-2 aboard the USS *Constellation* (CV-64) went off the side of the carrier during a night recovery. The S-3 reportedly suffered a brake failure after 'taking the wire'. The two crewmembers ejected safely.
- A US Navy F-14A of VF-154 'Black Knights' crashed on 1 April during a mission over southern Iraq due to mechanical failure. A Combat Search and Rescue (CSAR) team

BEHIND ENEMY LINES

Lucky escape

A three-ship formation of CH-47D Chinooks from F Company of the 159th Aviation Regiment was flying low over the Iraqi desert carrying troops and supplies to a new aviation base camp south of Baghdad.

As they flew near civilians, they suddenly noticed two men run over to a white pickup truck and pull out an AK-47 rifle and a hand-held rocket launcher.

'I felt a shudder in the aircraft, and a big boom' recalled one of the crew. The first missile had hit the sling load under the Chinook; the second hit the rear of the helicopter, but had luckily failed to detonate.

Two AK-47 rounds also hit them, with one penetrating an electrical panel behind the cockpit and the second hitting a strut in the cabin and grazing the cheek of one of the soldiers in the cabin.

Flying on and into a violent sandstorm, the three helicopters were eventually forced to set down their underslung loads of precious supplies to improve handling before trying to make it into the remote destination.

successfully recovered the pilot and Radar Intercept Officer (RIO) and took them to Ahmed al Jaber AB for treatment. Neither was seriously injured.
- A US Army AH-64 of the 1-3rd Aviation Regiment, 3rd ID (Mech), crashed in 'brown-out' conditions. The crewmembers were recovered safely.

2 April

- A US Navy F/A-18C Hornet of VFA-195 'Dambusters' from the USS *Kitty Hawk* (CV-63) was shot down near Karbala during a mission in support of Operation 'Iraqi Freedom'. Reports suggest the Hornet was possibly another victim of a US Patriot missile 'blue-on-blue' accident. The pilot, Lt Nathan 'OJ' White, was killed.

3 April

- A US Army UH-60 was brought down by small arms fire on 3 April near Karbala. Seven soldiers were killed, four injured.

Above: **Maintenance crews inspect a 172nd FS A-10A attached to the 392nd AEG after it was hit by an Iraqi SAM missile. Note the damage to the right engine, underlining the punishment the Thunderbolt II can take.** *USAF*

4 April

- A US Marine Corps AH-1W Cobra of HMLA-267/MAG-39, 3rd Marine Aircraft Wing, crashed near Al Aziziyal. Capt Benjamin W. Sammis and Capt Travis A. Ford were killed in action.
- Phoenix UAV ZJ402, British Army, shot down over Basra.
- Phoenix UAV ZJ417, British Army, shot down over Basra.

6 April

- A USAF 4th Fighter Wing F-15E Strike Eagle reported as being shot down near Tikrit. Both crew were killed.

8 April

- A USAF A-10A of the 110th FW, Michigan ANG, operating from a Forward Operating Base (FOB) was shot down near Baghdad. The pilot ejected safely and was picked up by US forces.
- A US Navy CH-46E crashed in the Eastern Mediterranean during a VERTREP operation for the USS *Harry S. Truman* (CVN-75). The crewmembers were recovered safely.

14 April

- A US Marine Corps AH-1W of MAG-39 was declared missing in central Iraq.

30 April

- A CH-53E assigned to HMH-465 suffered a hard landing and rolled over and caught fire near An Najaf. No injuries were reported.

9 May

- A US Army UH-60A Black Hawk operated by the 571st Medical Company (Air Ambulance) from Fort Carson, CO, crashed into the Tigris River near Samarrah. Three soldiers were killed in the incident, which was not a result of combat action.

19 May

- Four US Marines were killed in the crash of a CH-46E. The aircraft, which was assigned to HMM-364, crashed into a canal near Karbala.

26 May

- A US Army UH-60L was severely damaged on the ground in Iraq after being hit by a Bradley armoured vehicle.

12 June

- A US Army AH-64D helicopter assigned to the 101st Airborne Division was apparently shot down over western Iraq. The two crewmembers were not injured and were rescued immediately.

27 July

- Four crewmembers aboard a US Navy EA-6B Prowler ejected safely from the aircraft before it crashed into the Persian Gulf. The aircraft (BuNo 158800/NH-503, assigned to CVW-11) had just taken off from the deck of the aircraft carrier USS *Nimitz* (CVN-68).

14 August

- Two US Army aviators assigned to 1-4th Aviation were injured when their AH-64D suffered a hard landing during a maintenance test flight north of Tikrit.

2 September

- One US Army soldier was killed when a UH-60 crashed on take-off from Camp Dogwood in Baghdad.

23 October

- A US Army AH-64 crashed at Kirkuk airbase. The Apache broke in half, but the crew were unharmed (see below right).

25 October

- One of a pair of US Army UH-60L Black Hawks engaged in a reconnaissance mission in the vicinity of Tikrit was hit by a Rocket-Propelled Grenade (RPG). The aircrew was, however, able to perform a controlled emergency landing, but the Black Hawk subsequently caught fire and was destroyed. All five crewmembers escaped with only minor injuries.

29 October

- A US Army AH-64D was destroyed by fire in an incident that occurred in the 'Central Command area of operations'.

2 November

- A US Army CH-47 Chinook was shot down on killing 13 personnel on board. The Chinook was brought down by ground fire as it headed for Baghdad International Airport. Eyewitnesses reported seeing two shoulder-launched Surface-to-Air Missiles (SAMs) fired at the Chinook as it flew about 40 miles west of Baghdad.

7 November

- A US Army UH-60L assigned to the 5-101st Aviation crashed in Tikrit, after being hit by a Rocket-Propelled Grenade (RPG). Six soldiers aboard serial 92-26431 were killed.

15 November

- Two US Army UH-60Ls crashed near Mosul, shortly after sunset, killing 17 troops and injuring five. The crash was apparently the result of a mid-air collision that involved helicopters from the 4-101st AVN and 9-101st Aviation.

BEHIND ENEMY LINES

Scary landings

The Coalition helicopter fleet worked in gruelling conditions in the Iraqi deserts (and continues to do so). Despite reports of blinding sand, poor weather and enemy fire, the actual number of losses was surprisingly small.

The US Army suffered two AH-64 Apache incidents on 28 March. The AH-64A and AH-64D were from the 2-101st Avn, 101st Airborne Division 'Screamin' Eagles', and had been involved in attacks on the Medina Republican Guard Division near Karbala. The two separate crashes occurred as the helicopters operated from a desert Forward Operating Base (FOB) and were attributed to 'brown-out' conditions caused by clouds of sand kicked up as a helicopter approaches the ground. This makes it very difficult for the pilot to see the ground and some even consider it the most dangerous part of a mission. US Army pilots had trained for 'brown-out' landings extensively in the year leading up to deployment and also since arriving in-theatre in February. One Army spokesman described it as 'Literally the scariest thing I've done in my life'.

The first crash happened just minutes after the pilot had over-torqued the AH-64 during the take-off. The second helicopter crashed as it landed after completing its mission. Each crew escaped with minor injuries.

The situation with the 'brown-out' conditions and intense enemy fire had earlier forced 11th Avn Apaches to abandon attacks on the Medina Division on 24 March. It was during these missions that one Apache force-landed and its crew were captured by Iraqi troops.

Below: **This US Army AH-64 Apache suffered an emergency crash landing at Kirkuk airbase on 23 October 2003. The two crewmembers were unharmed.** *USAF*

22 November

- An A300B4 Freighter operated by the cargo carrier DHL was struck by a Surface-to-Air Missile (SAM) shortly after taking off from Baghdad International Airport. The aircraft was climbing through an altitude of 8,000ft (2,438m) when it was apparently struck by an SA-7 SAM. Although all hydraulic control was lost, and the aircraft's left wing was on fire, the crew managed to return to the airport using only differential engine thrust. After initially calling a missed approach, the crew landed heavily and ran off the runway into soft sand. No injuries were reported by the three-crew members, but the aircraft received significant damage both as a result of the missile strike and the emergency landing.

Above: The fuselage of a USAF A-10 is craned onto a shipping cradle to be ferried back to the US after it came under heavy enemy fire in April 2003 during OIF. *USAF*

- A US Army UH-60A crashed near Fallujah, while attempting to make an emergency landing. Four crewmembers and five soldiers aboard the Black Hawk were killed. The helicopter, which had been assigned to the 571st Medical Company and normally based at Biggs AAF, Fort Carson, CO, had been conducting a medical evacuation mission when the incident occurred.

9 December

- A US Army OH-58D suffered a hard landing following an apparent hit by a Rocket-Propelled Grenade (RPG). The Kiowa Warrior, which was assigned to the 1-82d Aviation came down near Fallujah, 35 miles (56km) west of Baghdad. Two crew members escaped injury, though the helicopter was destroyed by a post-landing fire.
- A USAF C-17A sustained a shoulder-fired SAM immediately after lifting off from Baghdad International Airport at dawn. The missile apparently struck one of the aircraft's four engines causing it to explode and slightly injure one of the 16 passengers and crew aboard the aircraft. The C-17A was assigned to the 62nd Airlift Wing and normally based at McChord AFB, WA.

10 December

- A US Army AH-64D was destroyed by fire after making a controlled emergency landing near a highway some 15 miles (24km) south of Mosul. The Apache, which was assigned to the 101st Airborne Division, may have been hit by ground fire and was on fire when it landed. Its two crewmembers were not injured.

2 January 2004

- A US Army OH-58D was shot down in Fallujah, killing one pilot and injuring the second. The incident, which occurred approximately 37 miles (60km) from Baghdad, involved an aircraft and personnel from the 1-82nd Aviation, operating as part of the 82nd Airborne Division.

8 January

- A USAF C-5 Galaxy was hit by ground fire as it departed Baghdad IAP. The aircraft, from the 60th Airlift Wing/22nd Airlift Squadron at Travis AFB, CA, returned safely to the airport.

13 January

- A US Army AH-64A operated by the 4-3rd Armored Cavalry Regiment was shot down approximately 10 miles (16km) north of Habbaniyah in western Iraq. Both crewmembers were rescued safely by a quick reaction force.

23 January

- Two crewmembers aboard a US Army OH-58D were killed when it crashed northwest of Qayyarah in northern Iraq. The crew was assigned to the 101st Airborne Division and the 10th Infantry Division.

25 January

- An OH-58D, assigned to the 10th Infantry Division's 3-17th Cavalry, crashed into the Tigris River in Mosul, killing both crewmembers. The helicopter had been involved in a Search and Rescue (SAR) mission.

25 February

- A US Army OH-58D of O Troop of the 4th Squadron, 3rd Armored Cavalry Regiment (O/4-3rd ACR) crashed into a river near Habbinayah, killing both crewmembers.

BEHIND ENEMY LINES

Hog down

One of the only fixed-wing victims of Iraqi fire was a USAF A-10A Thunderbolt II, which was shot down near Baghdad IAP on 8 April. The pilot, from the 110th FW, Michigan ANG, ejected safely and was recovered by ground forces. He was reported to be in good health. The A-10A was actually from the 190th FS, Idaho ANG, and was operating from an undisclosed location. Brig Gen Vincent Brooks, deputy operations director at CENTCOM, said '(We) believe it was hit by a SAM'. Another CENTCOM official confirmed the 'Hog' appeared to have been shot down by Iraqi forces. Due to the kind of operating environment encountered during the type's missions, other USAF 'Hogs' sustained multiple hits. But, thanks to the type's legendary survivability, they were able to safely return to base.

Right: This A-10 shows signs of damage from an Iraqi SAM that exploded near the aircraft. *USAF*

After the Storm: Re-building Iraq

After combat operations officially ceased, Coalition forces engaged in the re-building of the infrastructure and services of Iraq. However, the country remained extremely dangerous with terrorist insurgents still inflicting casualties upon Coalition forces as well as native Iraqis who were perceived to have supported the efforts to put the nation on a path towards democracy.

The most prolific breakthrough in post-war Iraq came on 13 December 2003 when Saddam Hussein was dramatically captured alive by US and Coalition Special Forces in his hideout near Tikrit. A news conference held by US Administrator in Iraq Paul Bremer and Lt Gen Ricardo Sanchez gave details of Operation 'Red Dawn', the mission to capture Saddam, following the receipt of intelligence to pinpoint his possible location.

Top left: **A strong contingent of Coalition aircraft stayed in the Gulf region after the main combat phase of OIF officially ceased. This photo illustrates the force in-situ at one base in late December 2003, with a USAF KC-135R leading a 366th Wing F-15E Strike Eagle from Mountain Home AFB, a pair of Aviano-based 31st FW F-16CGs and two RAF Tornado GR4s.** *USAF*

Left: **Having missed out on the main combat phase of OIF, RAF Lakenheath's 494th EFS deployed to the region in mid-2003 to assume the combat air support mission.** *USAF*

Above: **Two 192nd FW, Virginia ANG F-16Cs maintain patrol high over the Iraqi desert.** *USAF*

The operation involved assets from the 4th Infantry Division as well as 'Coalition Special Forces' (including Kurdish fighters) and air cover from US Army attack helicopters and USAF aircraft. The US Army led an assault on two possible hideout locations – dubbed 'Wolverine 1' and 'Wolverine 2'. A compound near the rural farmhouse at 'Wolverine 2' in Ad Dawr was found to have a camouflaged 'Spider Hole' as Lt Gen Sanchez described it. On investigation this was found to be a 6-8ft hiding hole with a small room at the bottom – with Saddam Hussein found 'tired and dishevelled' inside. He reportedly put up no resistance and 'not one shot was fired'. Saddam was found along with $750,000 in cash, a number of light arms and two assistants nearby.

Subsequent intelligence revealed that Saddam had gone on the run as Baghdad fell into Coalition hands. He headed north to Tikrit and used a succession of safe houses as he eluded forces tracking him down. Some reports suggested he had rallied his supporters at public meetings, and had even visited the graves of his sons Uday and Qusay on the day they were buried following their deaths at the hands of US forces. Saddam's capture sent a clear message to his loyal followers that times were changed for good in Iraq.

Top left: Missions flown after the cessation of the air war are taking aircrews to all areas of the country in support of the ground forces that remain in-theatre. This RAF Lakenheath-based 494th EFS F-15E patrols over Baghdad during a late-2003 deployment. *USAF*

Centre left: A 48th FW F-15E fires off a salvo of decoy flares as it comes off the tanker and heads for a target over Iraq. *USAF*

Left: The RAF Tornado GR4 detachment at Ali al Salem continues to provide vital air cover for British and Coalition assets still busy inside Iraq. Note the RAPTOR pod underneath the fuselage of this example. *Denis J. Calvert/Inter Air Press*

Top: British troops take a breather from the tireless task of helping maintain stability in the Basra area. *Jeremy Flack/API*

Above: F-15E pilot Maj Grant 'Doctor' Bucks of the 494th EFS checks for traffic as he follows his flight lead out for a combat support mission over Iraq. *USAF*

Right: The tiger caged. Saddam Hussein was captured by the 1st Brigade Combat Team, 4th Infantry Division on 13 December 2003. *US DoD*

US Navy